FOR ORGANS, PIANOS & ELECTRONIC KEYBOARDS

30 *Classical* MASTERWORKS

18

D0613696

ISBN 978-1-4950-3086-4

HAL•LEONARD® CORPORATION
7777 W. BLUEMOUND RD. P.O. BOX 13819 MILWAUKEE, WI 53213

Visit Hal Leonard Online at
www.halleonard.com

Contents

Andante Cantabile
from SYMPHONY NO. 5

Registration 8
Rhythm: Fox Trot

By Pyotr Il'yich Tchaikovsky

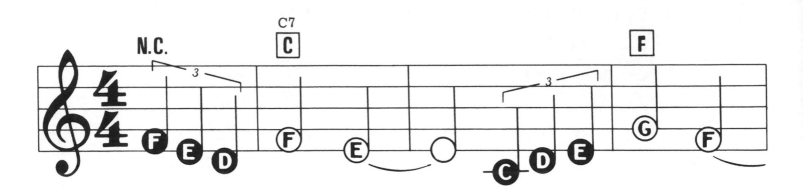

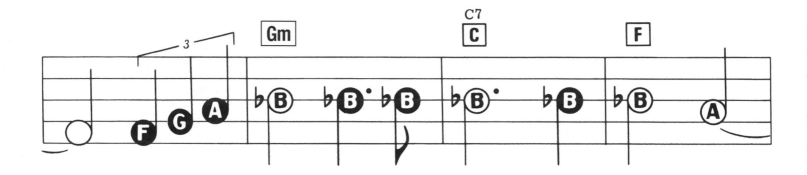

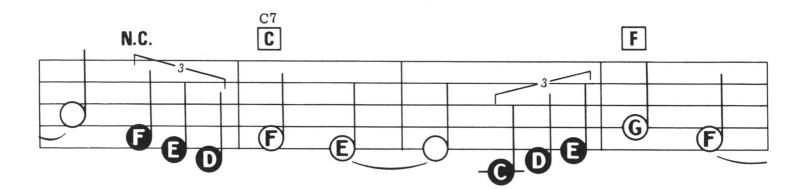

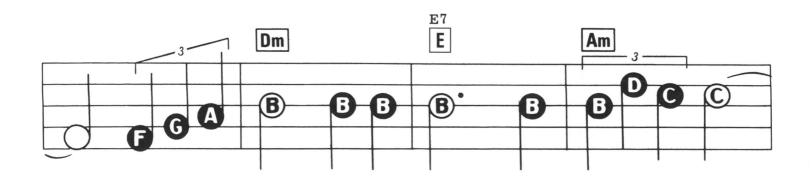

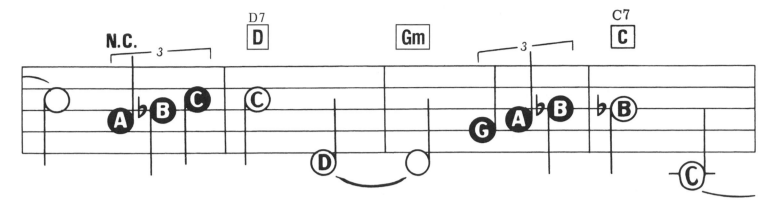

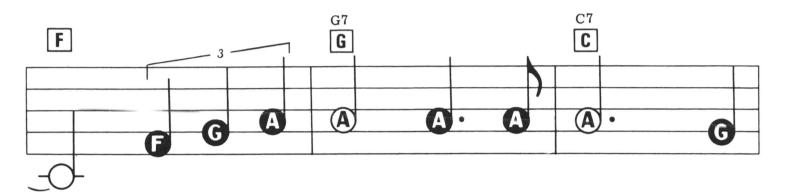

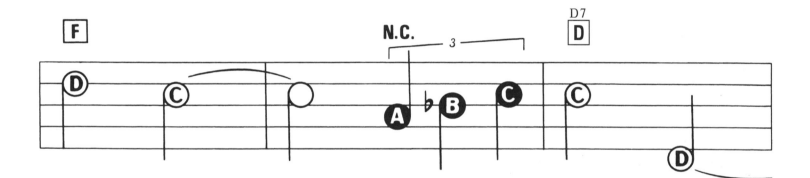

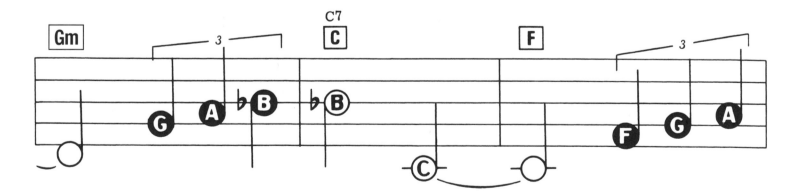

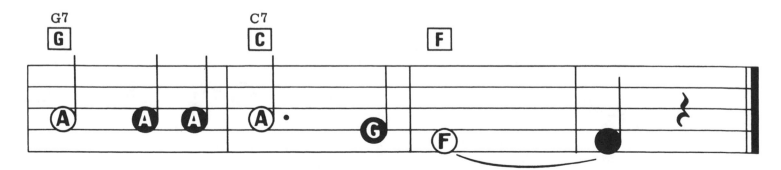

Artist's Life

Registration 3
Rhythm: Waltz

By Johann Strauss, Jr.

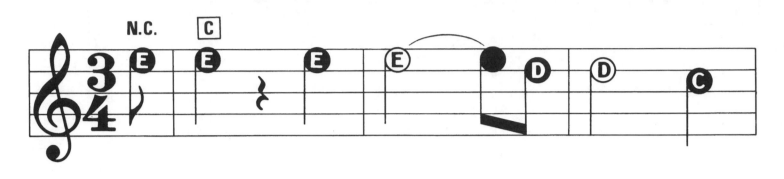

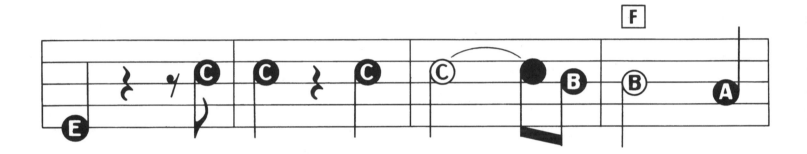

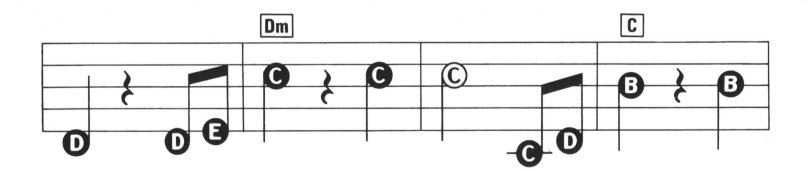

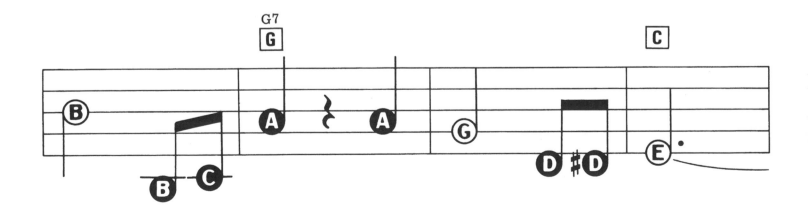

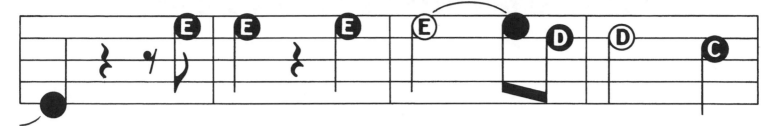

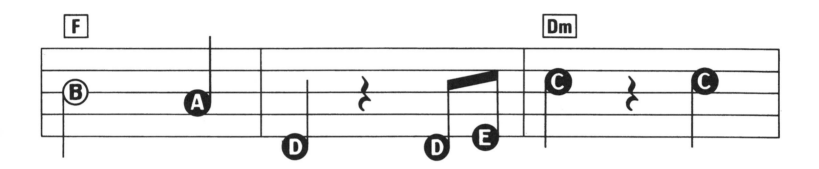

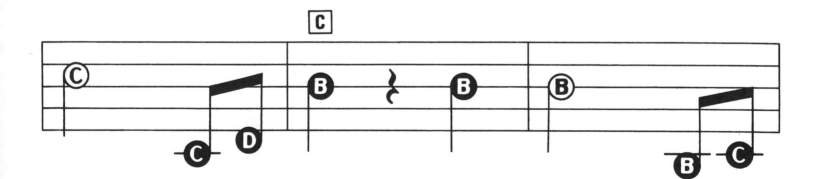

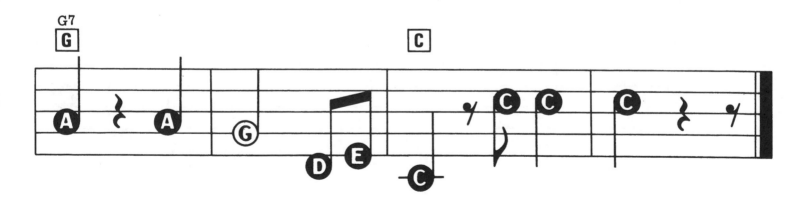

By the Beautiful Blue Danube

Registration 2
Rhythm: Waltz

By Johann Strauss, Jr.

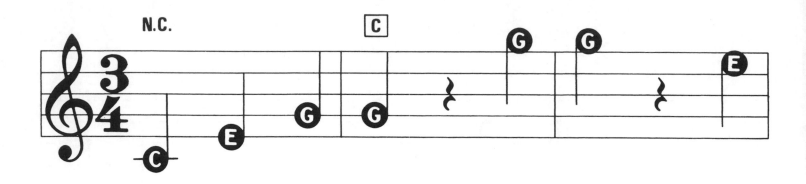

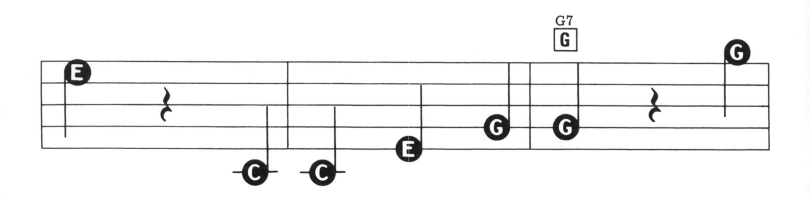

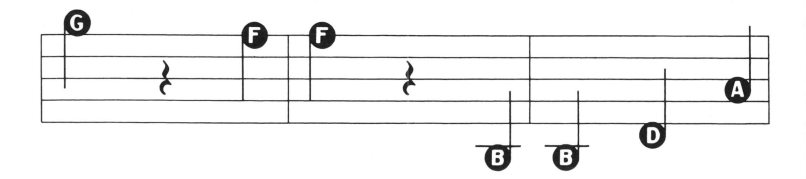

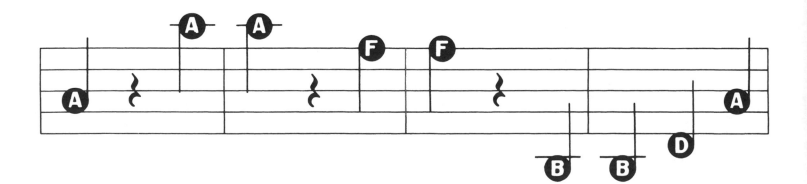

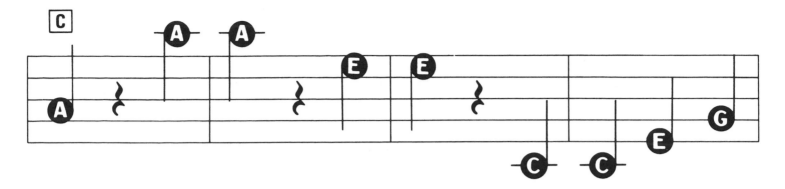

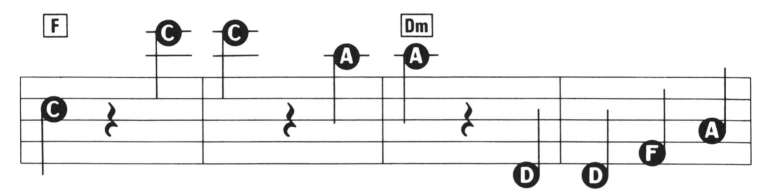

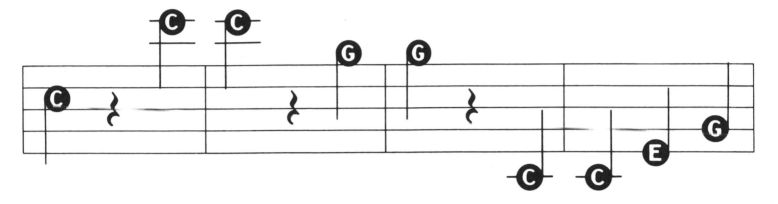

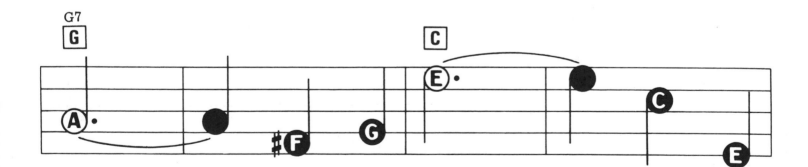

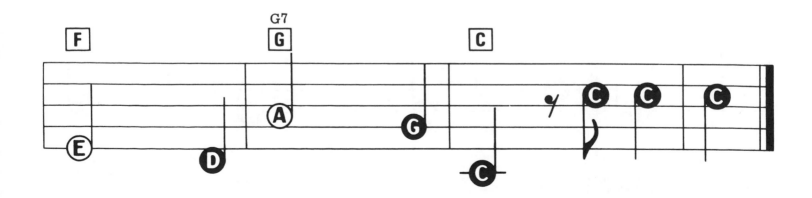

Capriccio Italien

Registration 2
Rhythm: Waltz

By Pyotr Il'yich Tchaikovsky

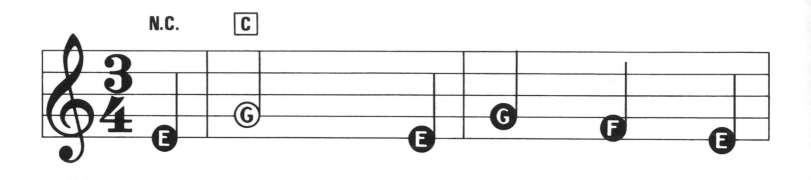

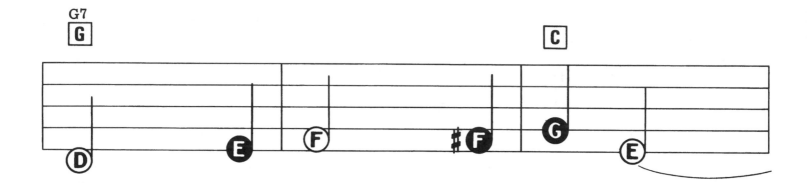

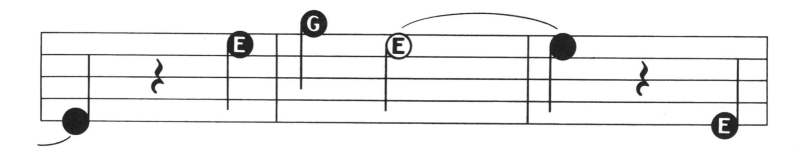

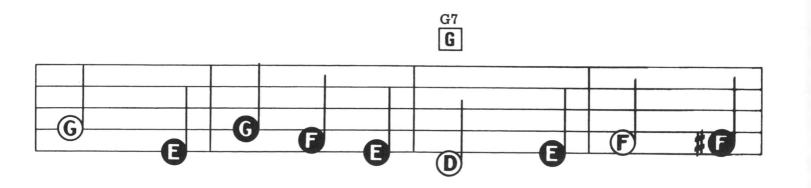

11

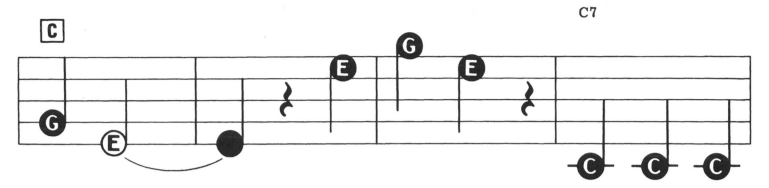

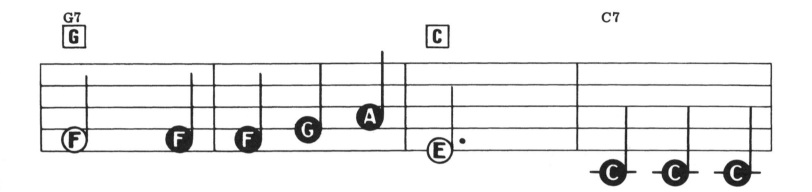

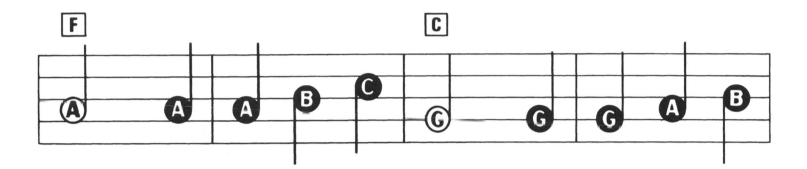

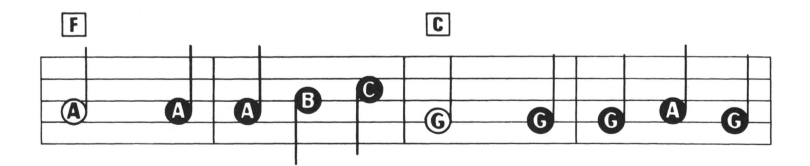

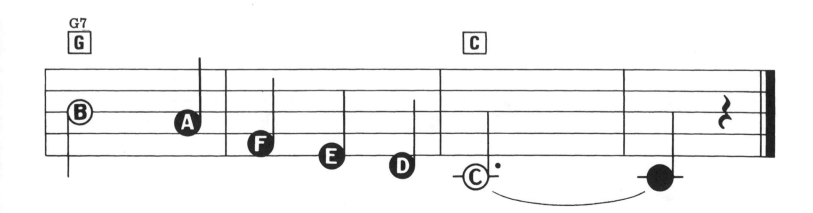

Clair de Lune

Registration 8
Rhythm: Waltz or None

By Claude Debussy

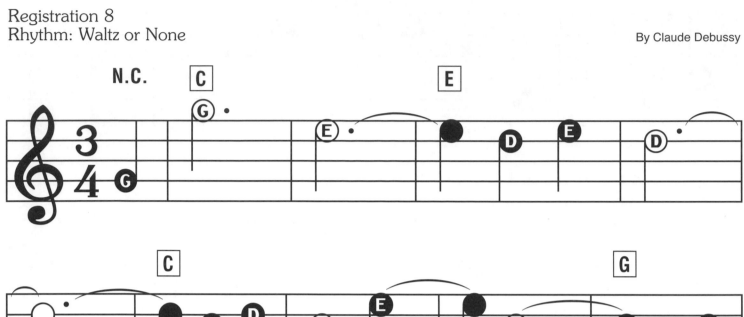

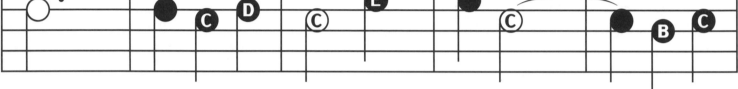

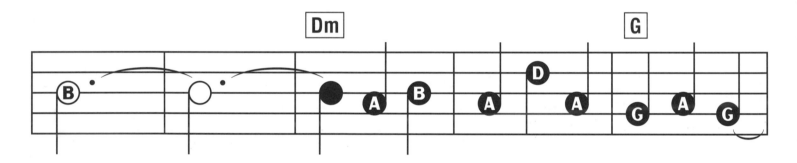

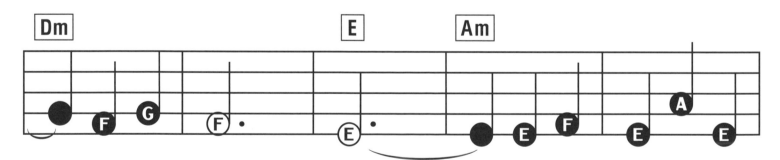

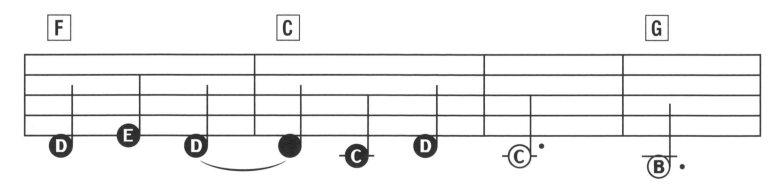

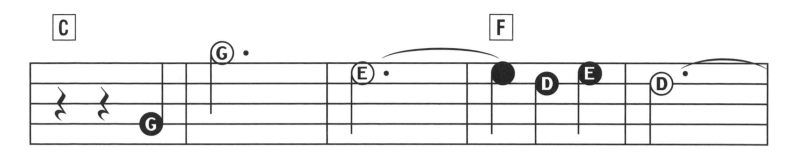

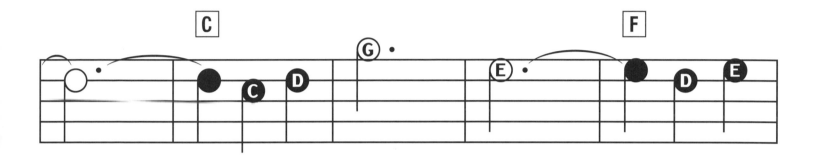

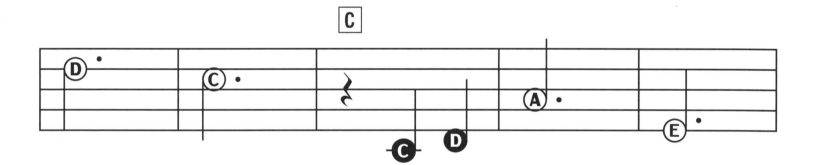

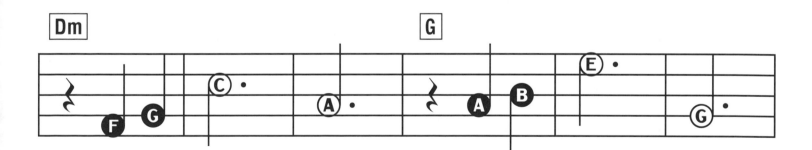

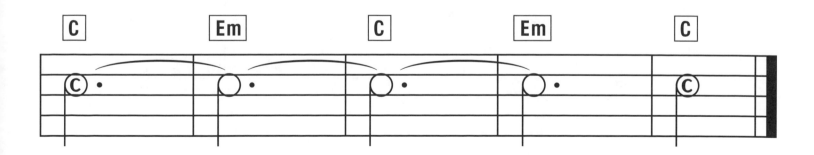

Emperor Waltz

Registration 3
Rhythm: Waltz

By Johann Strauss, Jr.

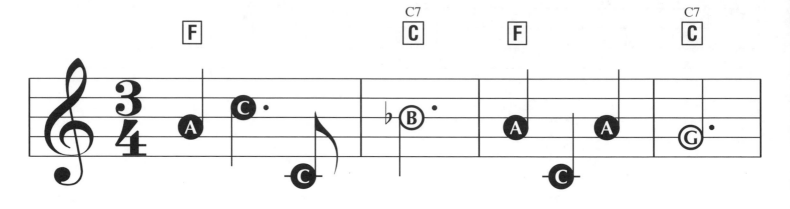

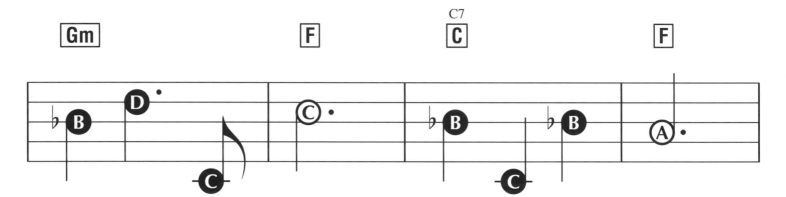

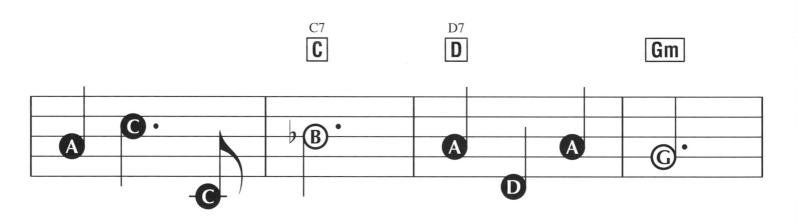

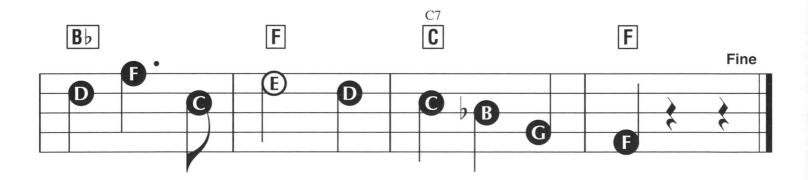

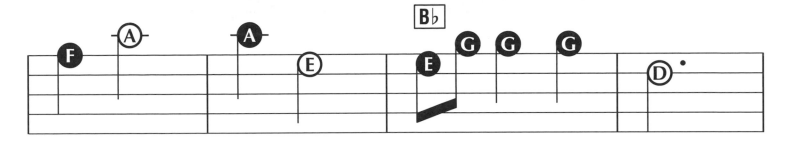

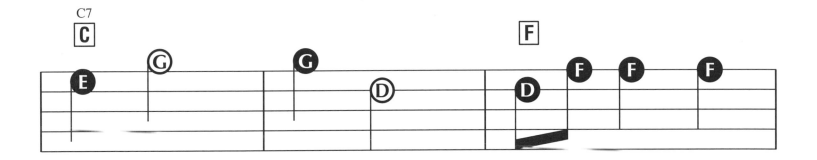

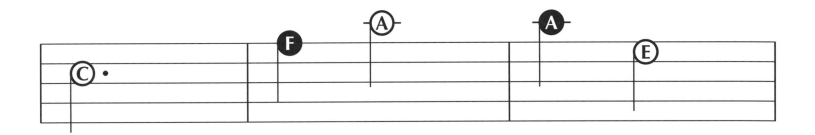

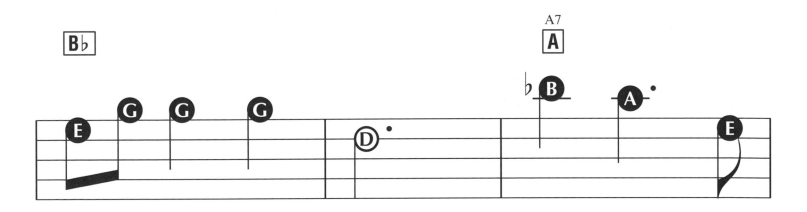

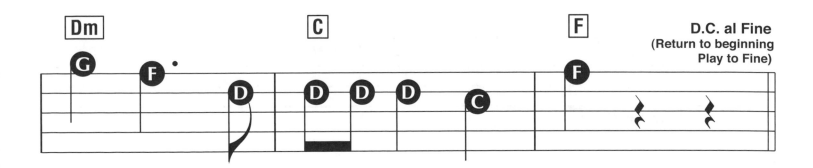

D.C. al Fine
(Return to beginning
Play to Fine)

Fantaisie-Impromptu

Registration 8
Rhythm: None

By Frederic Chopin

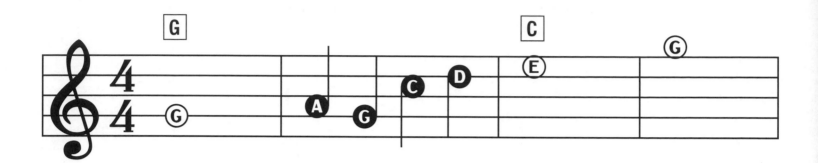

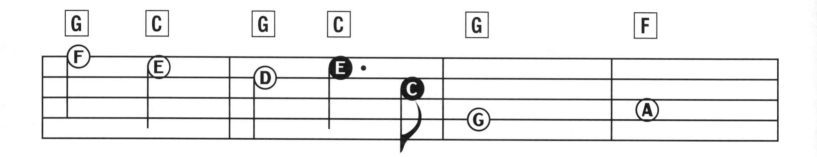

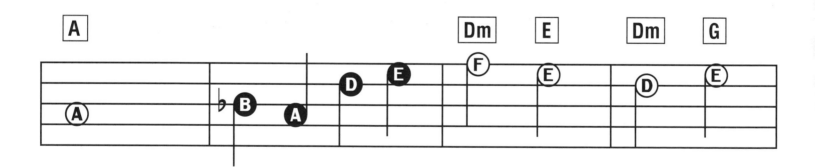

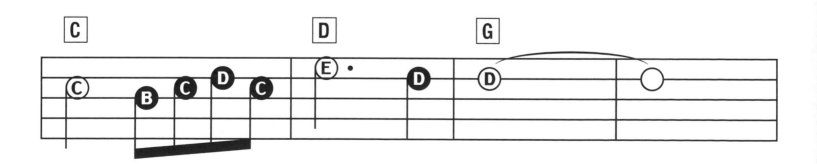

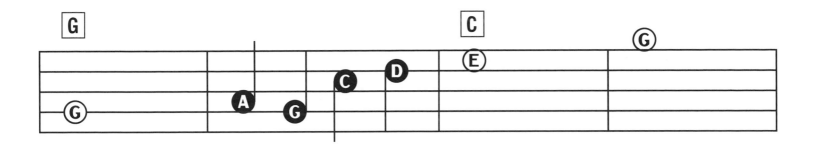

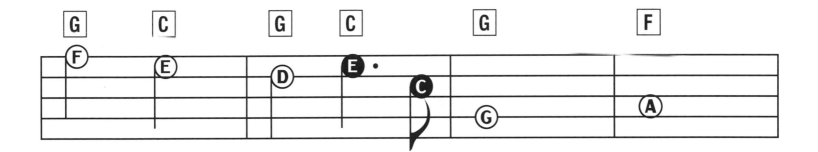

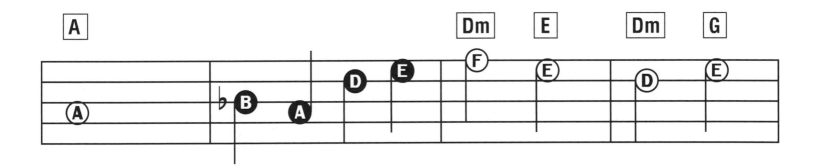

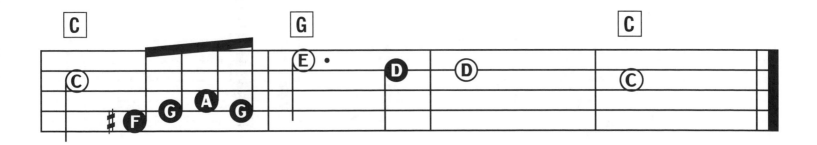

Für Elise

Registration 8
Rhythm: Waltz or None

By Ludwig van Beethoven

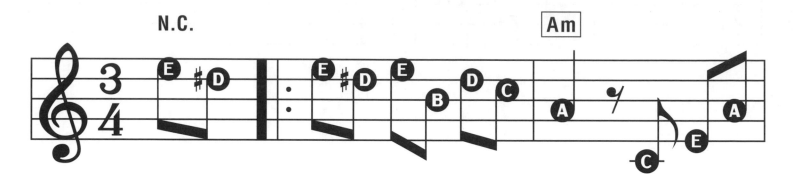

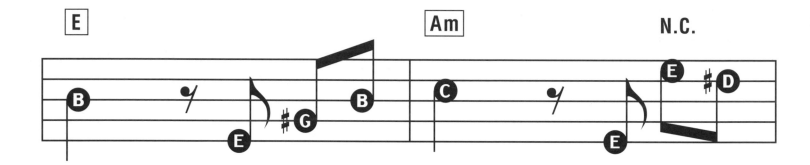

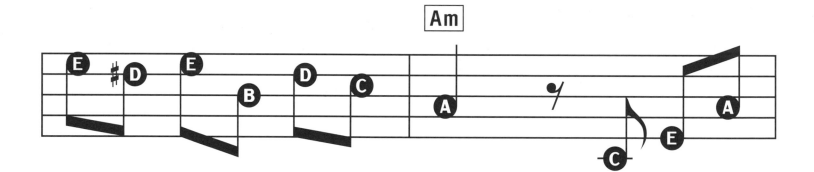

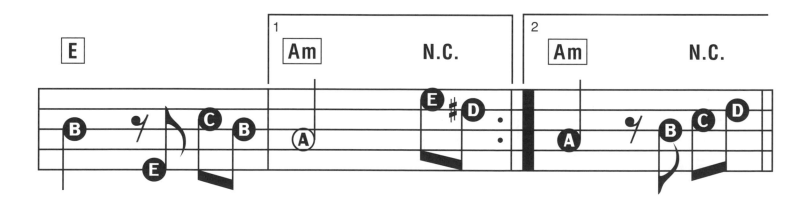

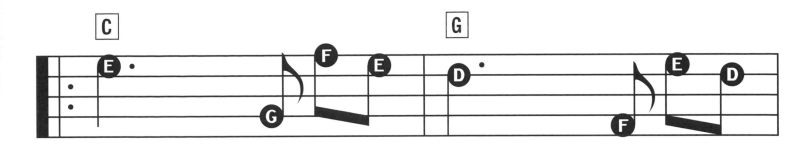

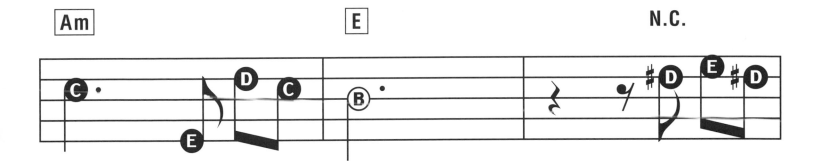

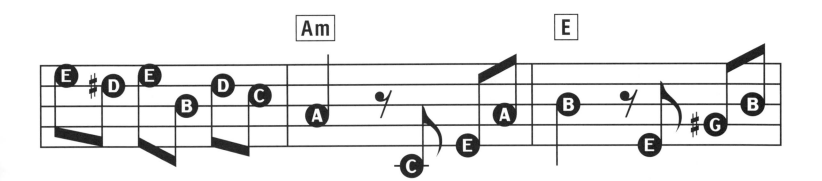

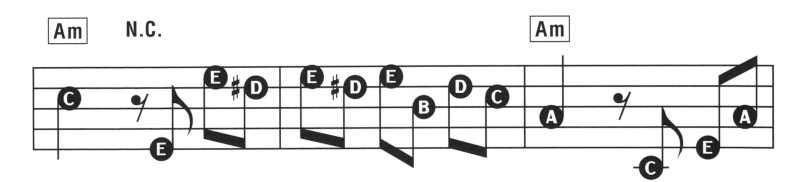

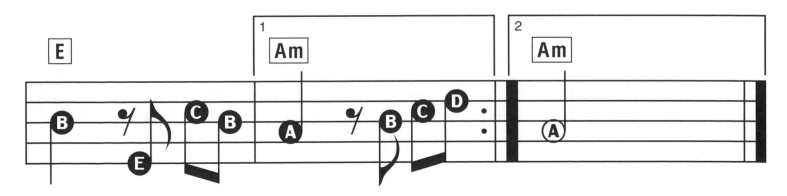

Humoresque

Registration 8
Rhythm: Fox Trot

By Antonin Dvořák

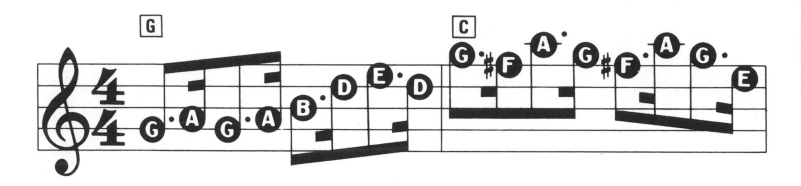

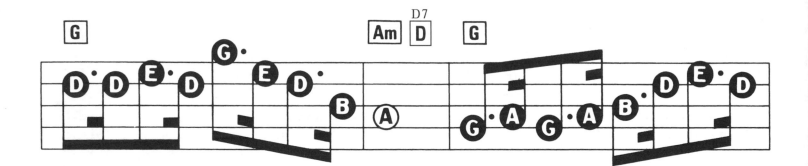

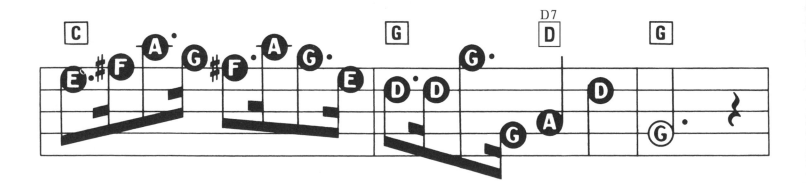

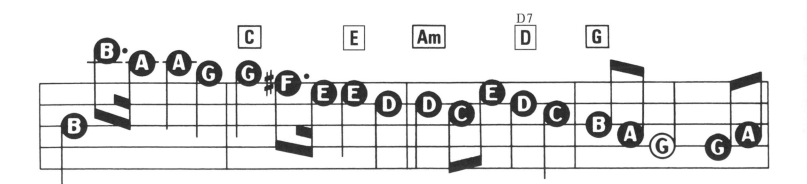

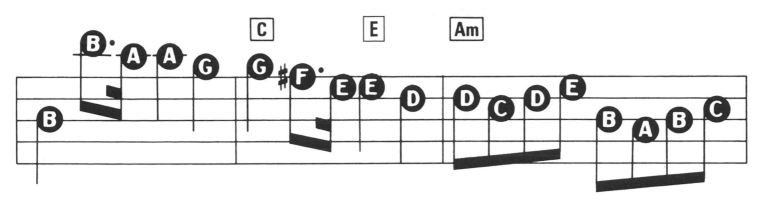

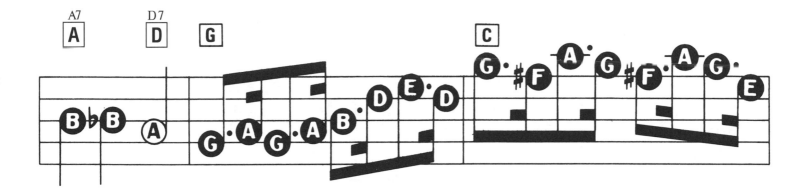

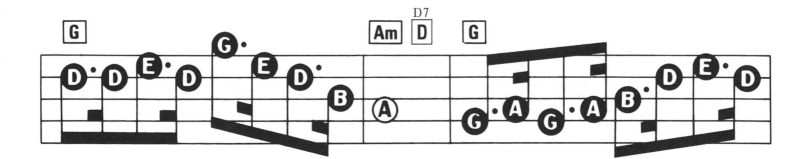

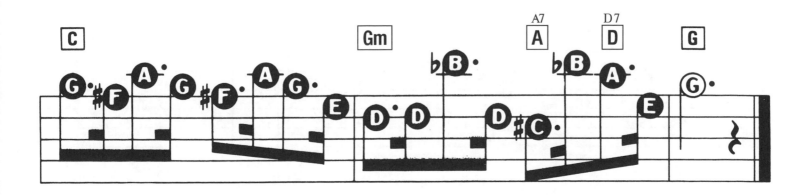

Intermezzo
from CAVALLERIA RUSTICANA

Registration 3
Rhythm: Waltz or None

By Pietro Mascagni

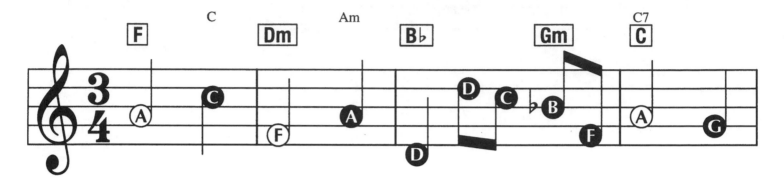

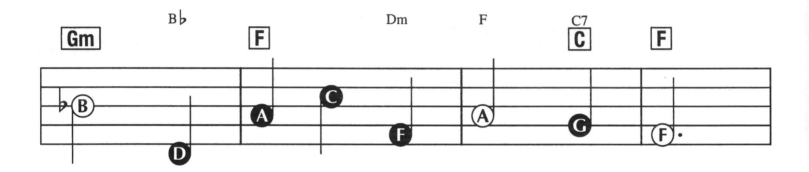

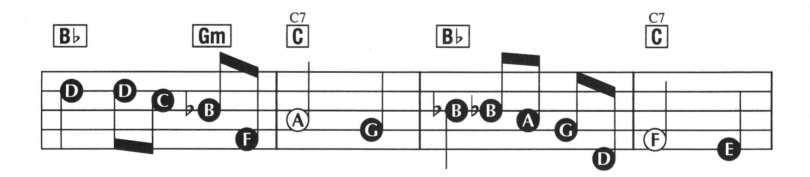

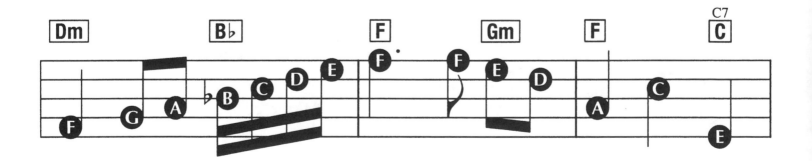

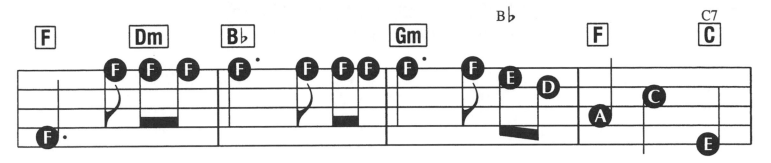

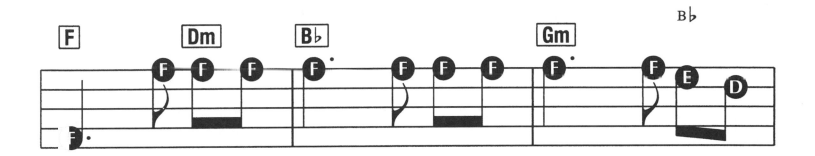

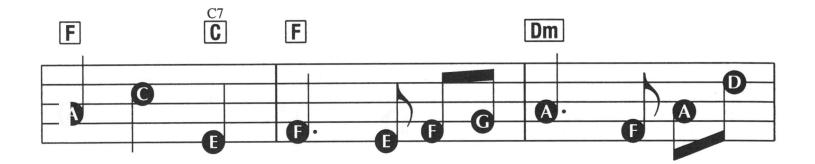

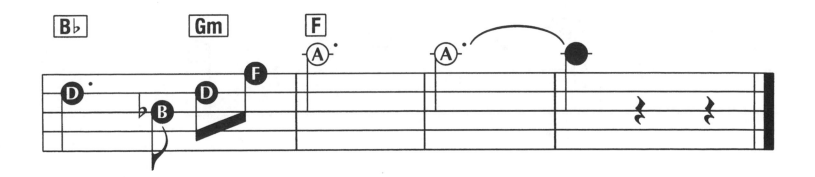

Juliet's Waltz Song
from ROMEO AND JULIET

Registration 3
Rhythm: Waltz

By Charles Gounod

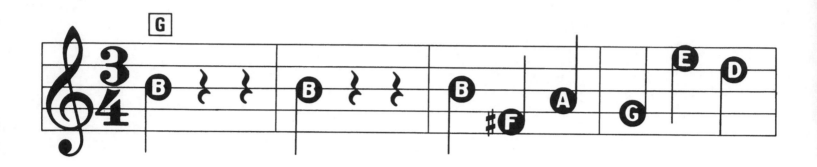

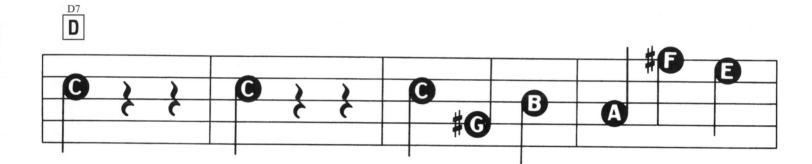

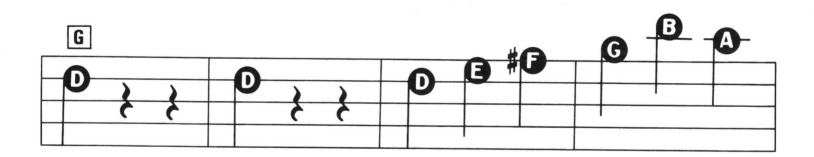

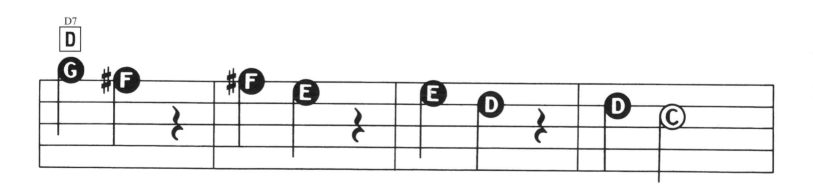

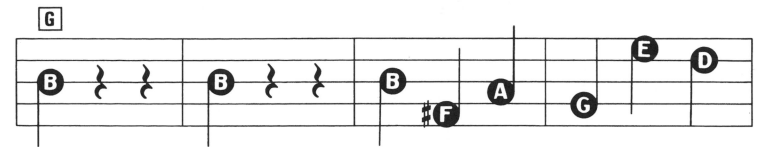

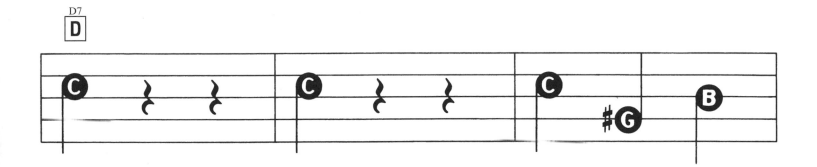

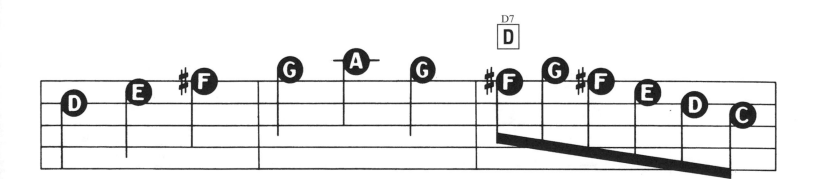

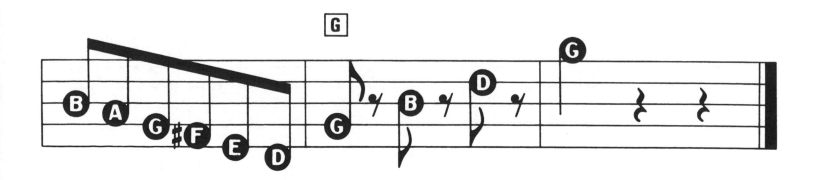

Liebestraum
(Dream of Love)

Registration 8
Rhythm: Waltz

By Franz Liszt

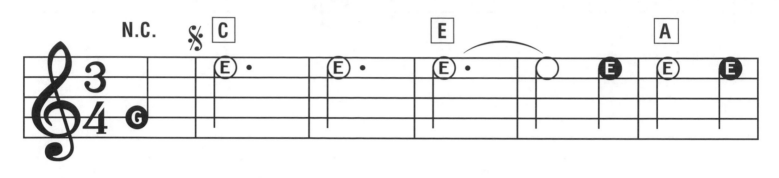

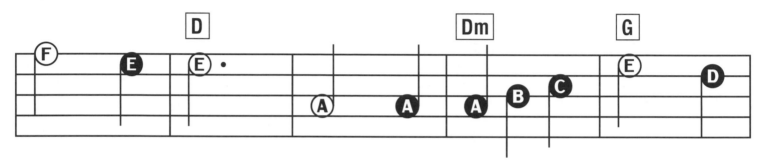

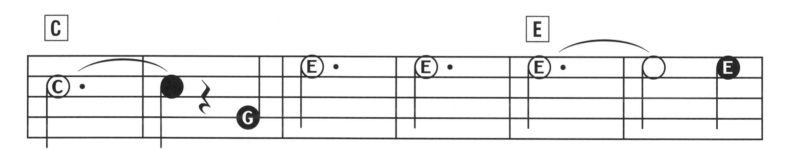

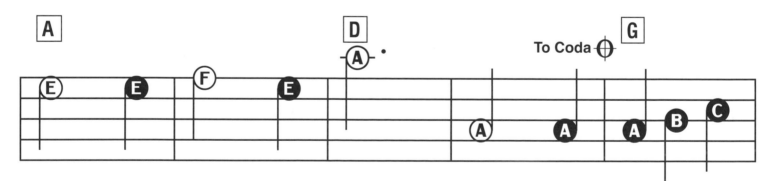

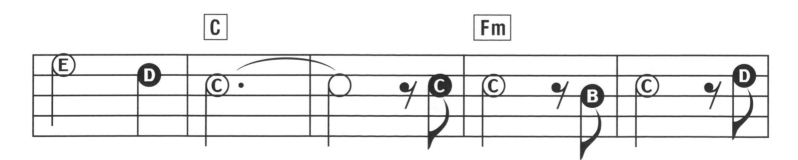

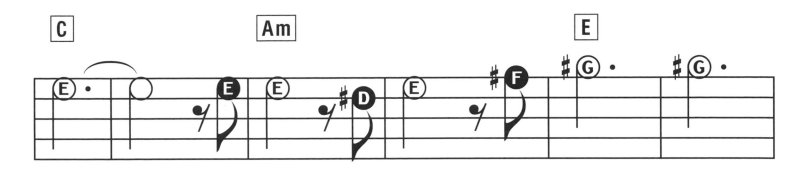

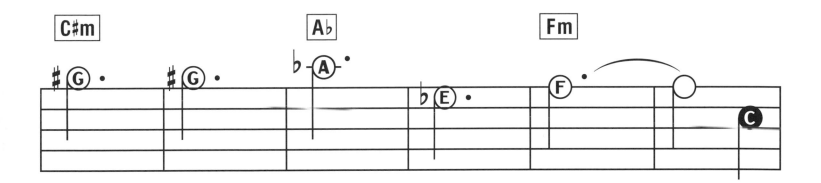

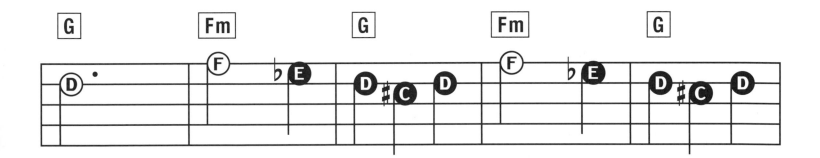

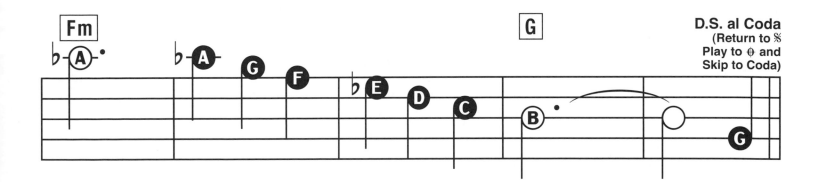

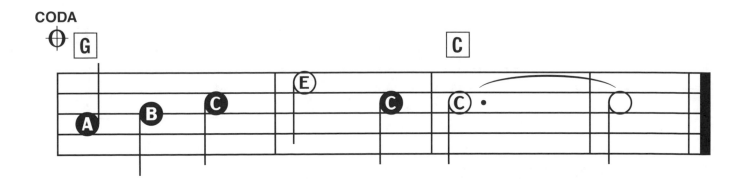

Lullaby
(Wiegenlied)

Registration 10
Rhythm: Waltz

By Johannes Brahms

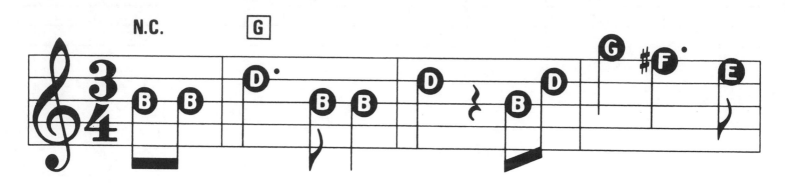

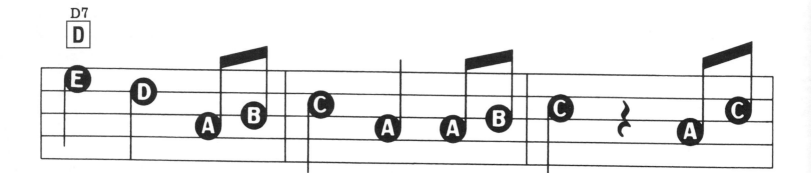

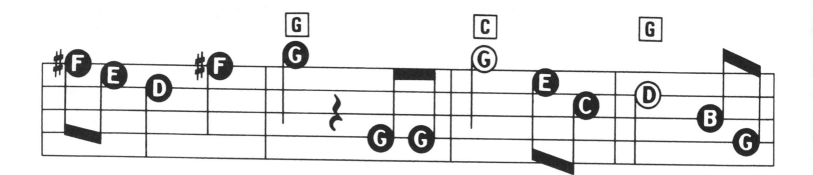

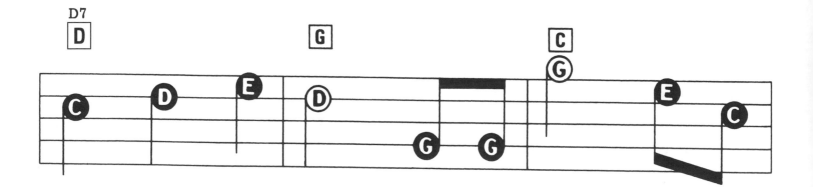

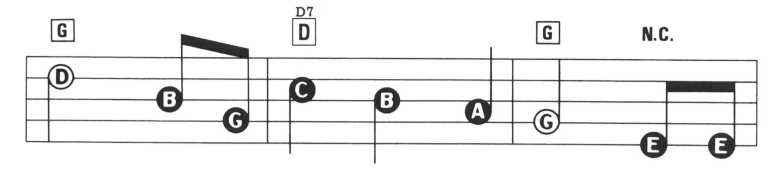

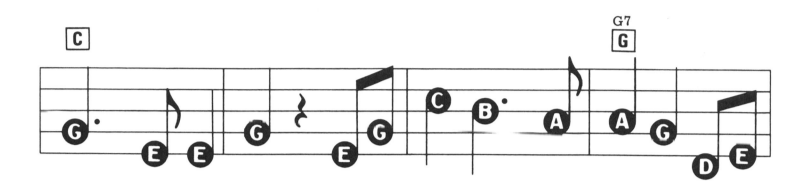

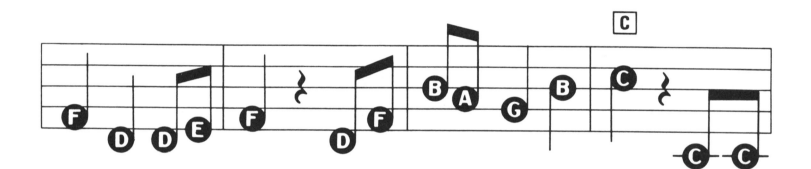

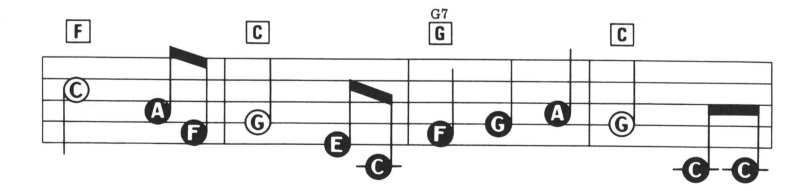

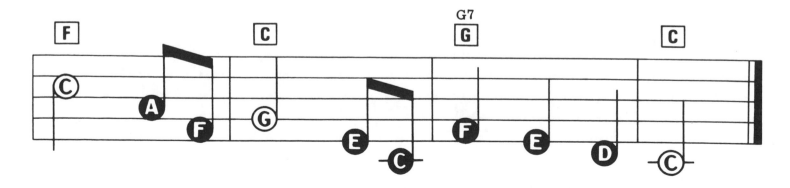

Mattinata

Registration 3
Rhythm: Waltz

By Ruggero Leoncavallo

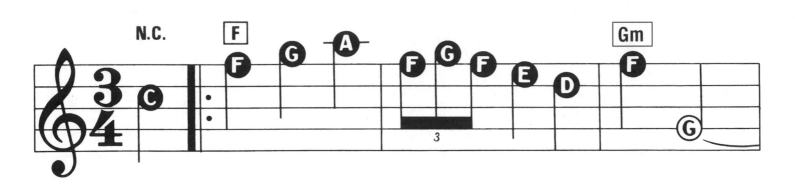

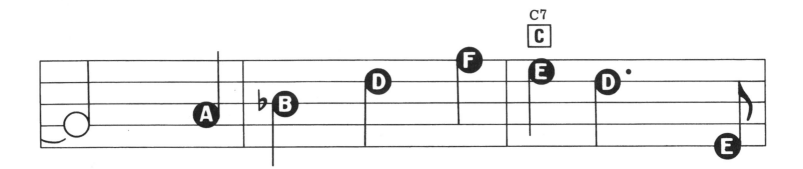

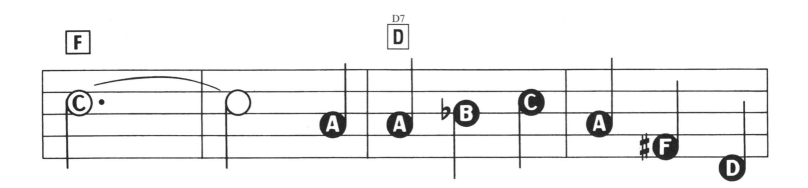

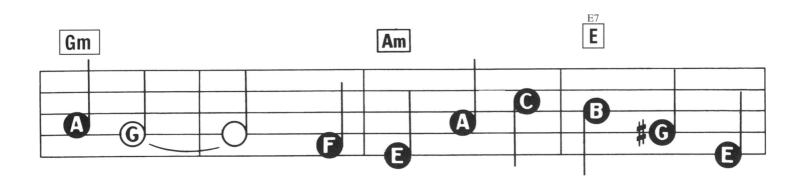

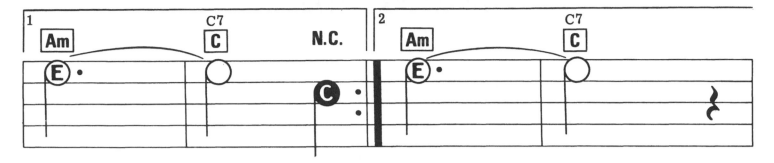

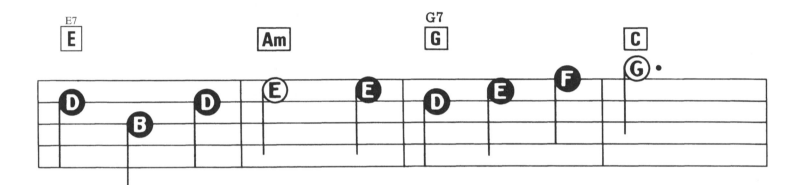

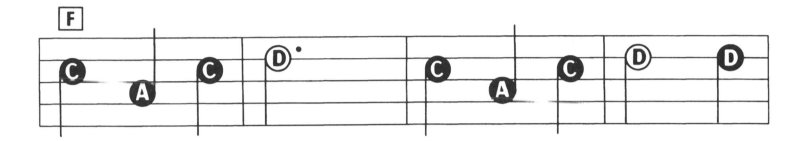

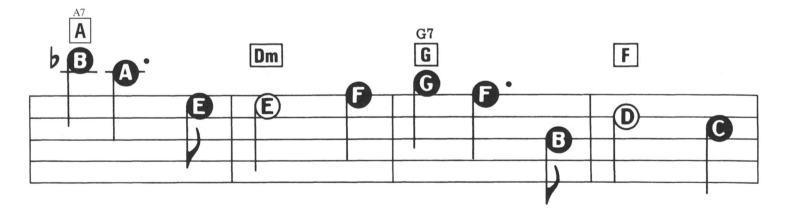

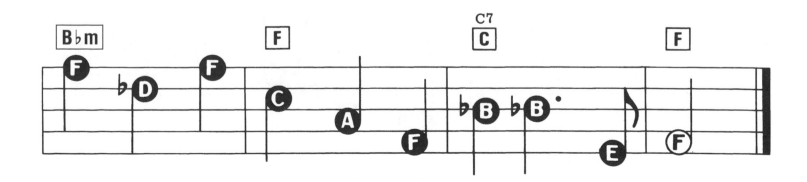

Meditation
from THAÏS

Registration 3
Rhythm: Ballad

By Jules Massenet

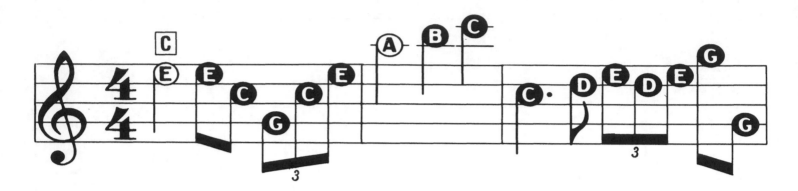

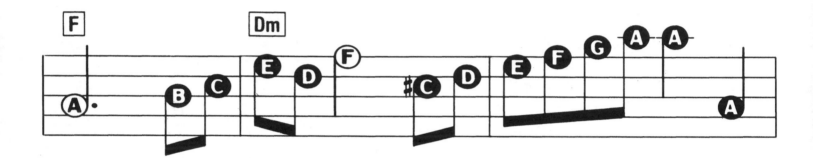

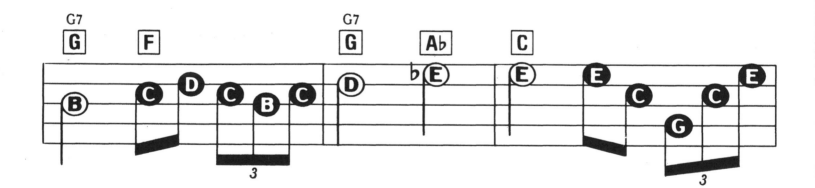

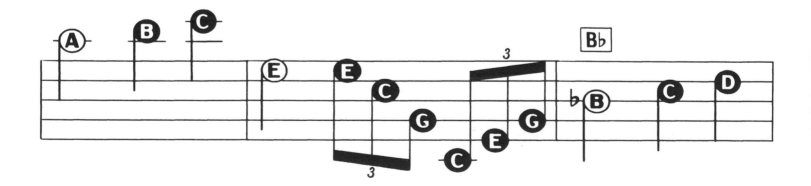

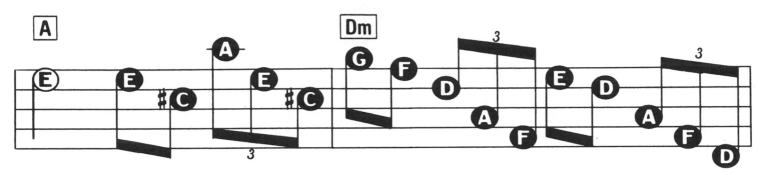

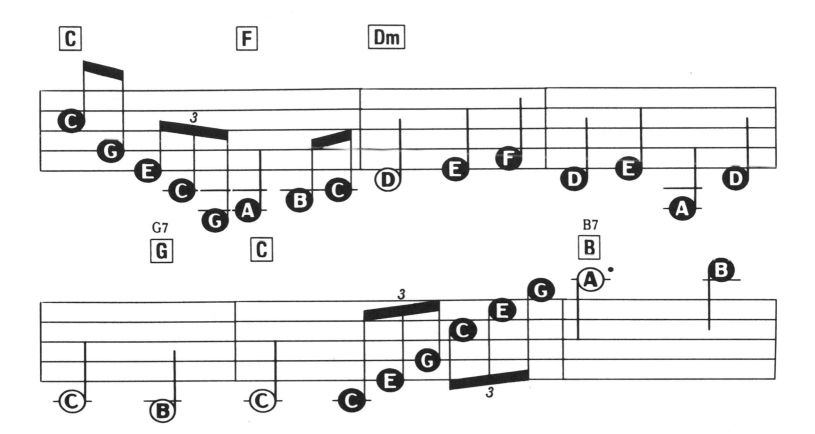

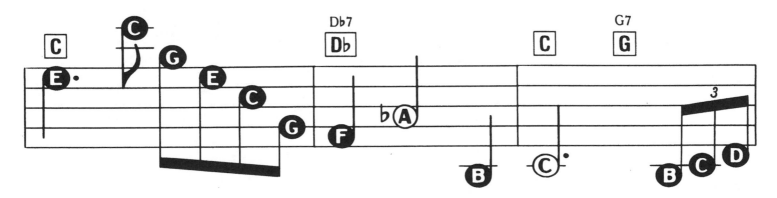

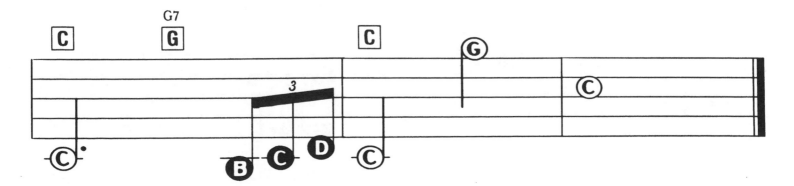

Minuet
from DON GIOVANNI

Registration 3
Rhythm: Waltz

By Wolfgang Amadeus Mozart

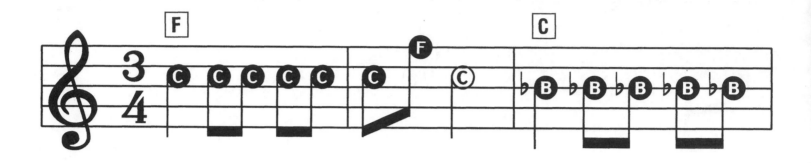

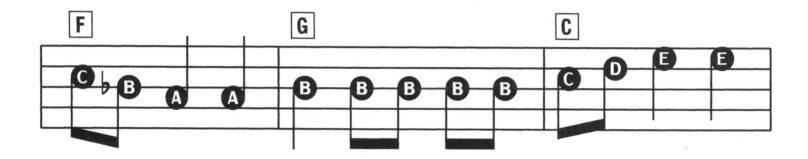

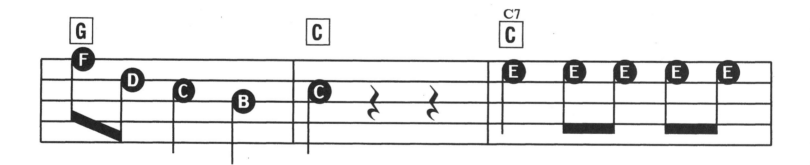

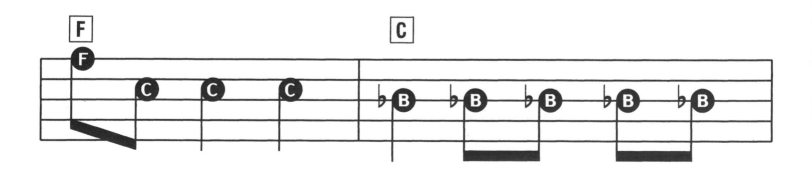

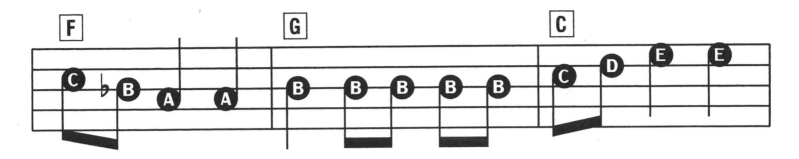

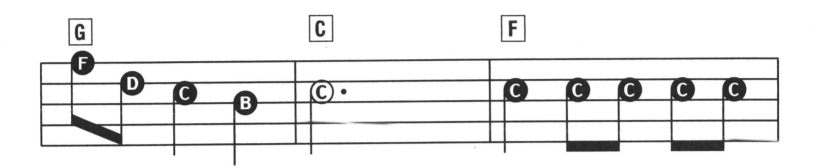

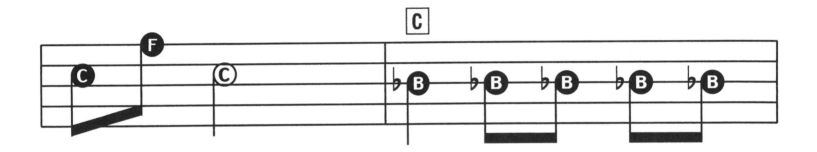

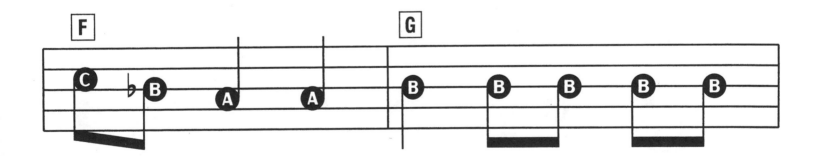

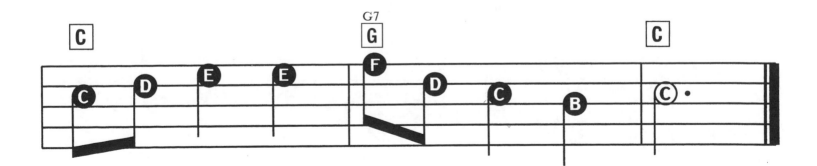

Nocturne

Registration 8
Rhythm: Waltz

By Frédéric Chopin

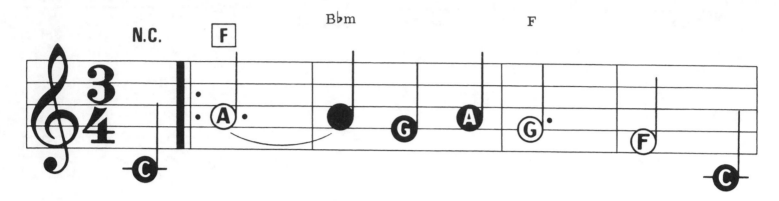

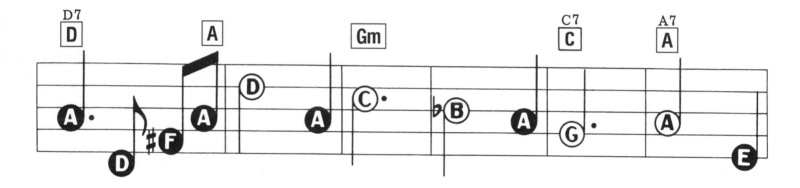

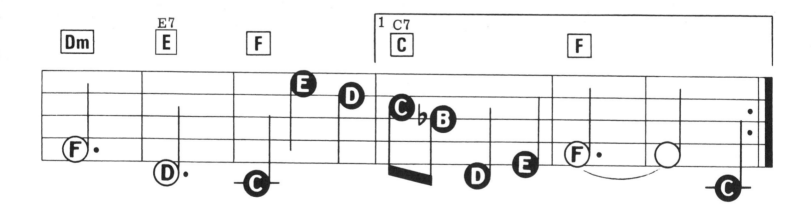

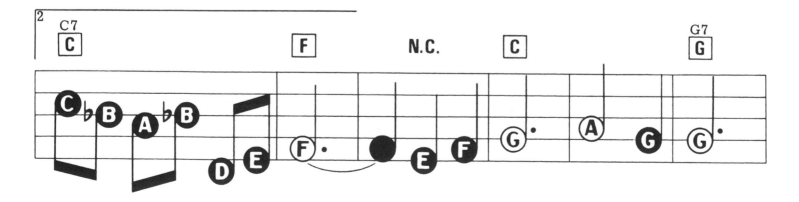

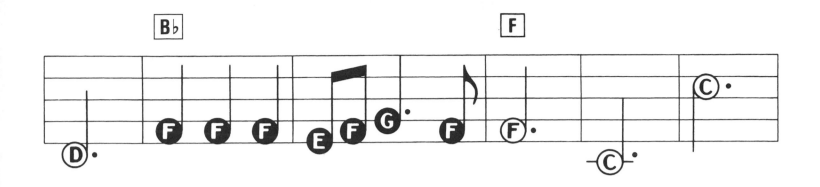

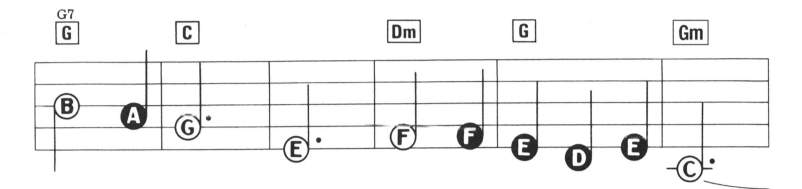

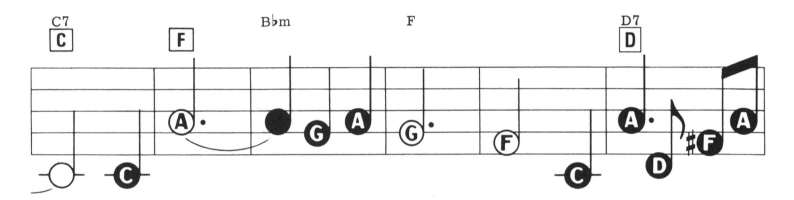

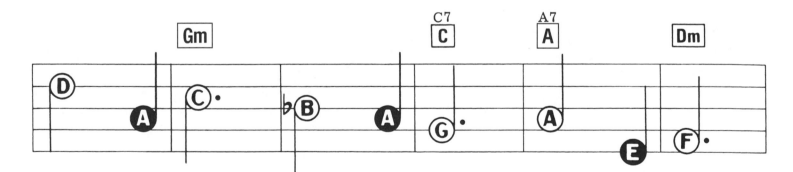

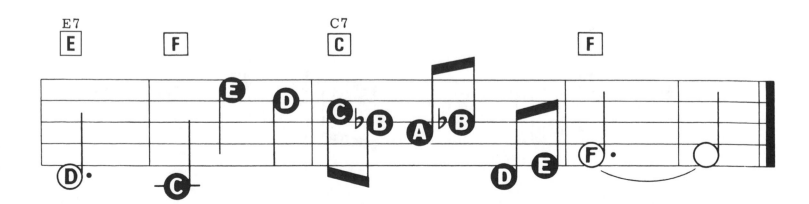

Pilgrims' Chorus
from TANNHÄUSER

Registration 6
Rhythm: Waltz

By Richard Wagner

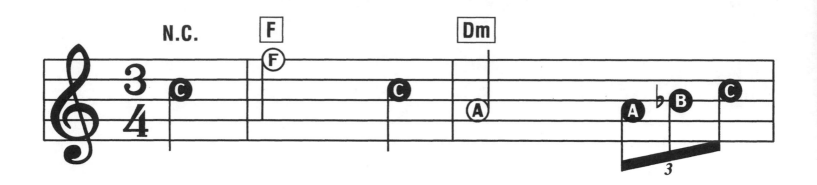

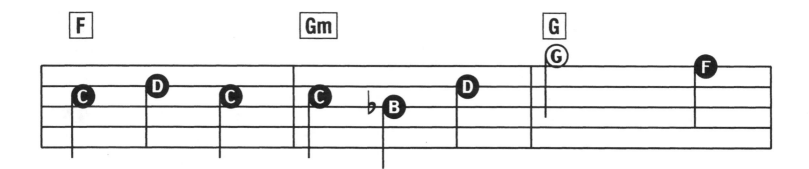

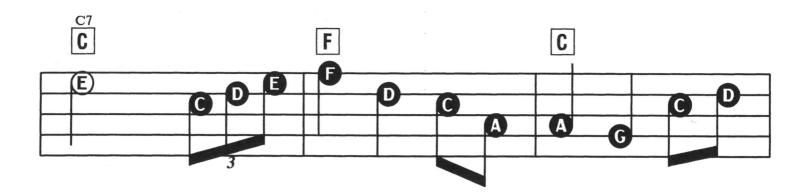

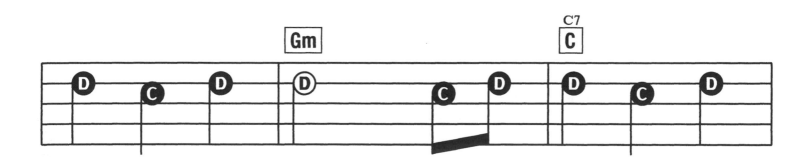

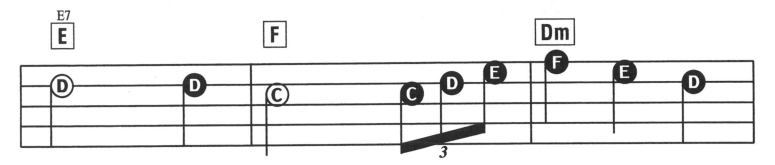

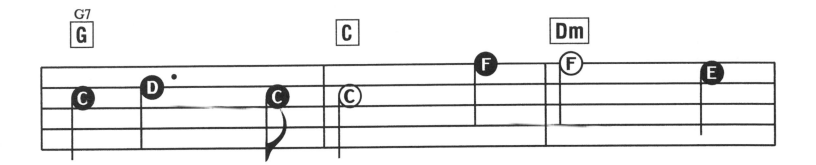

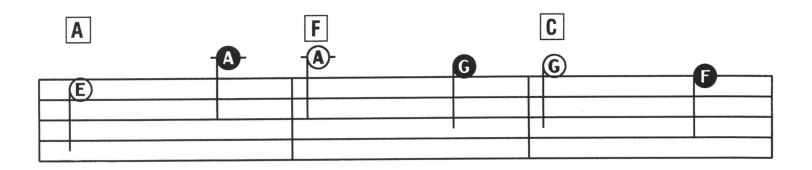

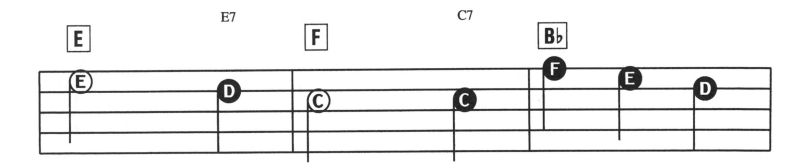

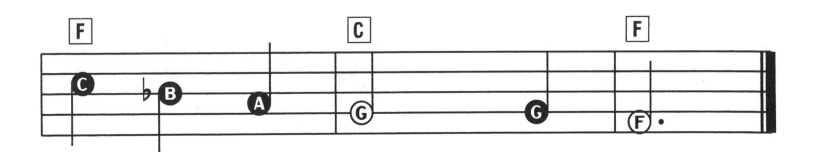

Poet and Peasant Overture

Registration 10
Rhythm: Waltz

By Franz von Suppe

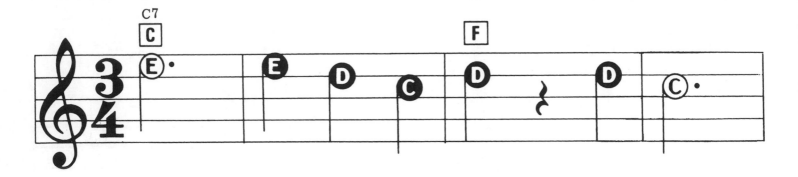

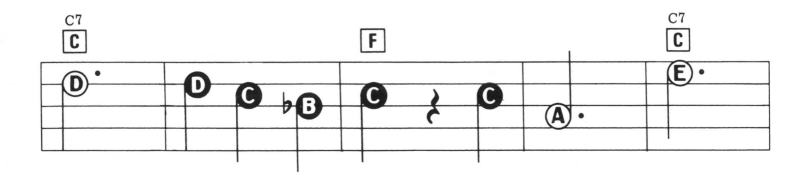

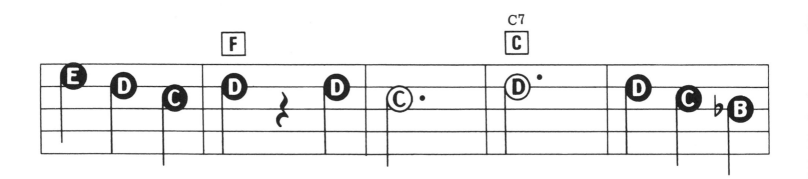

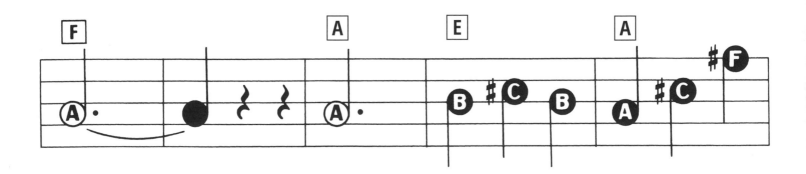

41

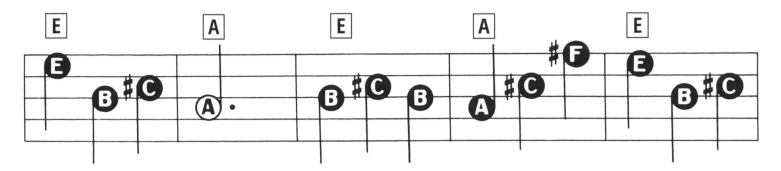

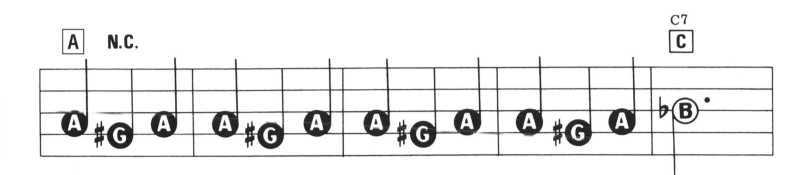

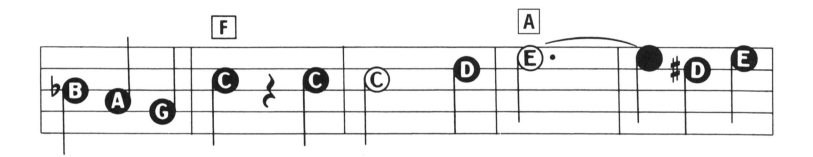

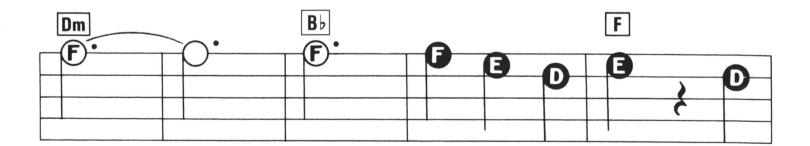

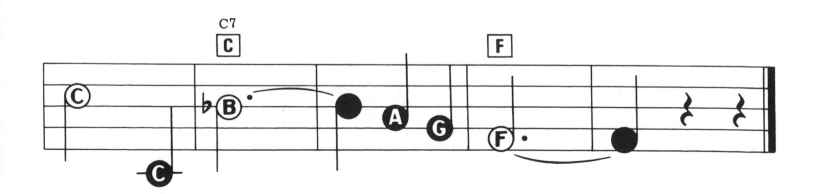

Rêverie

Registration 8
Rhythm: Fox Trot or Ballad

By Claude Debussy

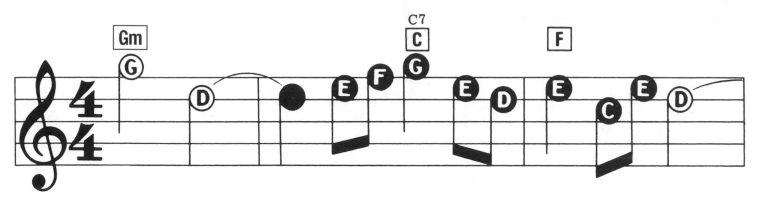

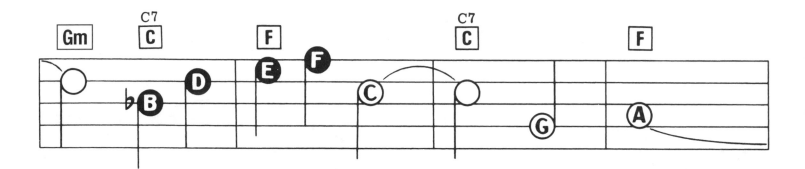

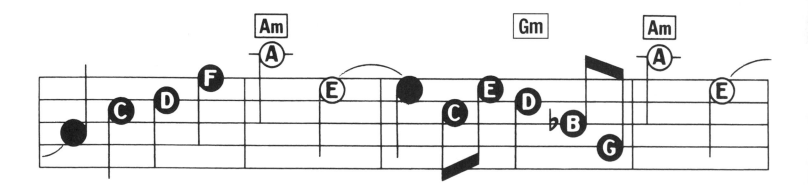

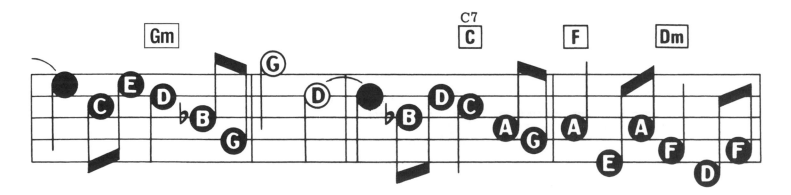

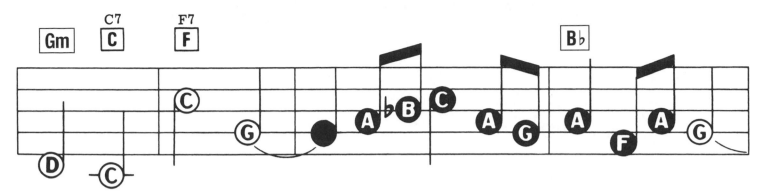

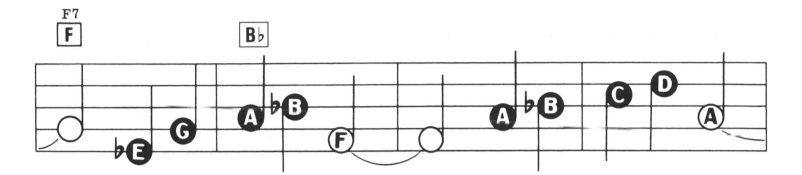

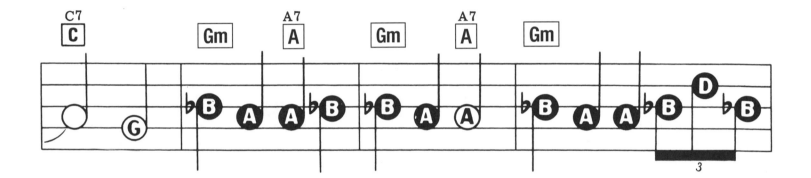

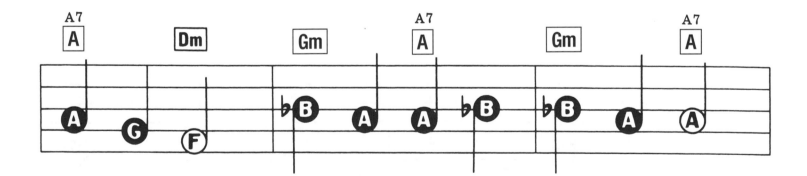

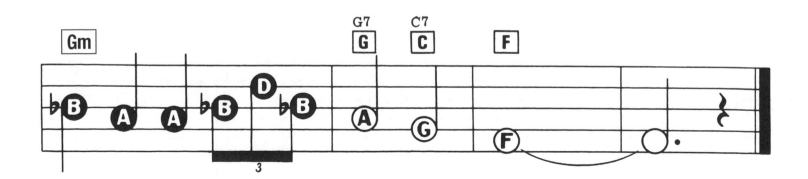

43

Ride of the Valkyries
from DIE WALKÜRE

Registration 2
Rhythm: Waltz

By Richard Wagner

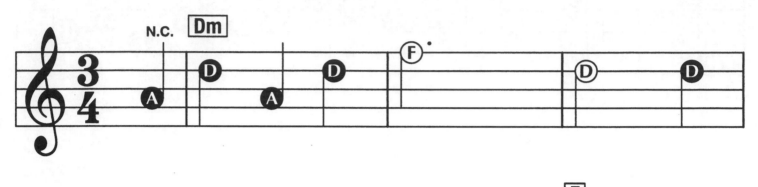

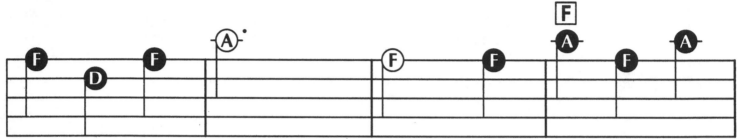

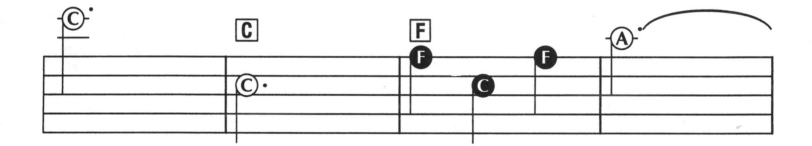

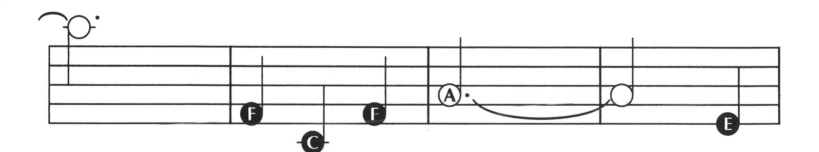

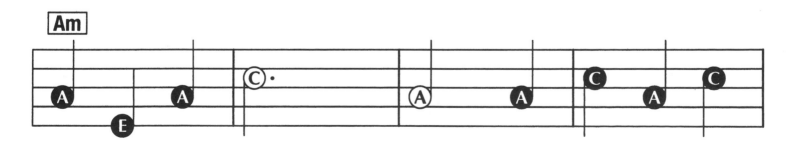

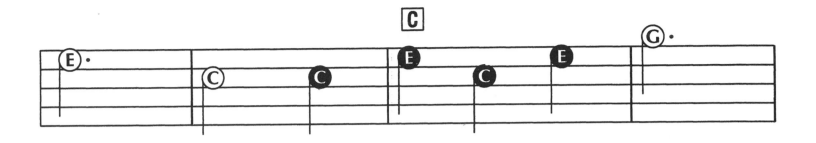

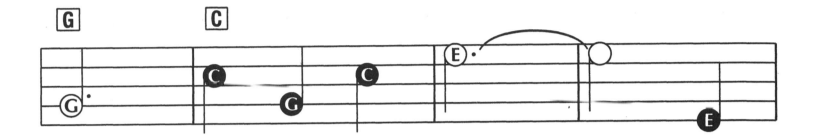

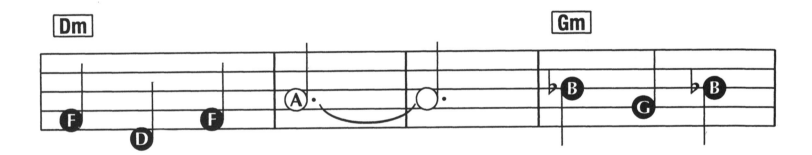

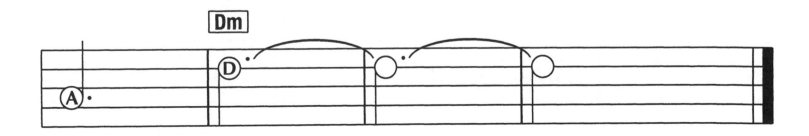

Romeo and Juliet
(Love Theme)

Registration 3
Rhythm: Ballad

By Pyotr Il'yich Tchaikovsky

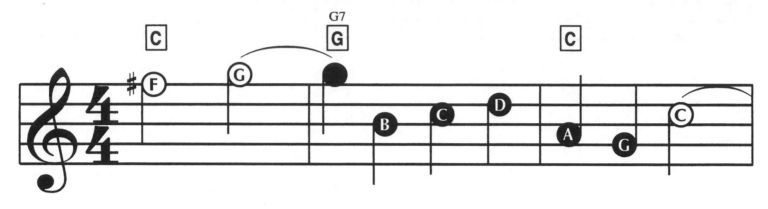

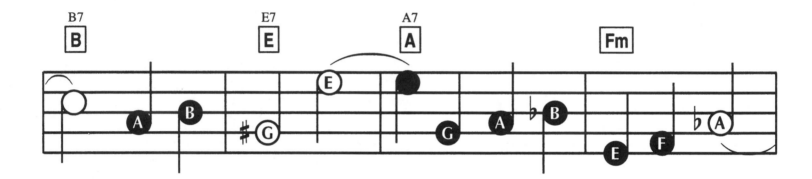

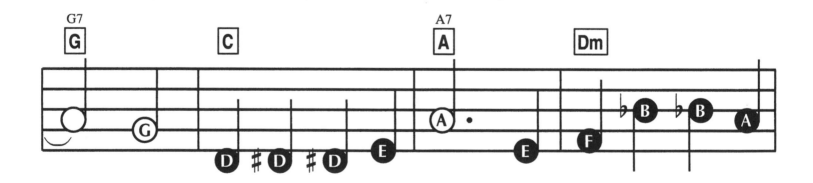

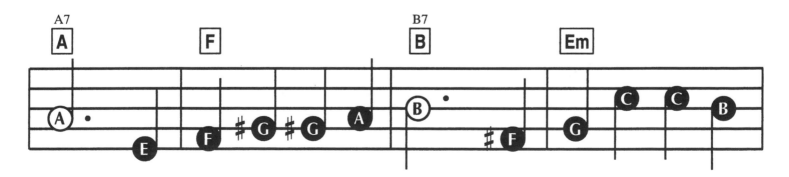

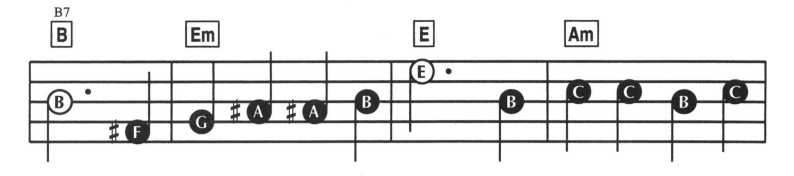

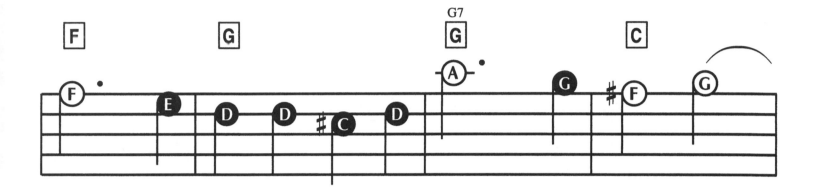

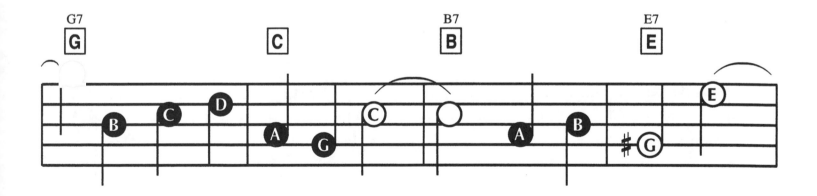

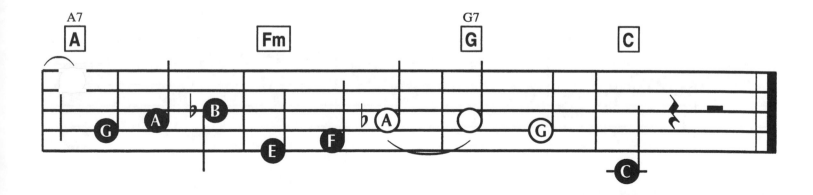

Serenade
(Ständchen)

Registration 8
Rhythm: Waltz

By Franz Schubert

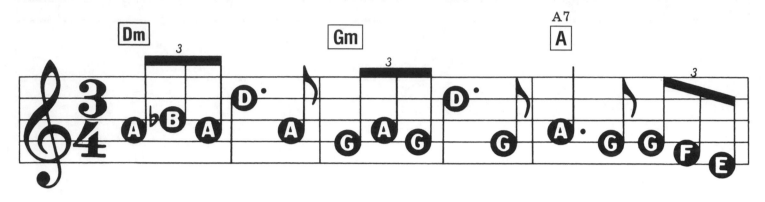

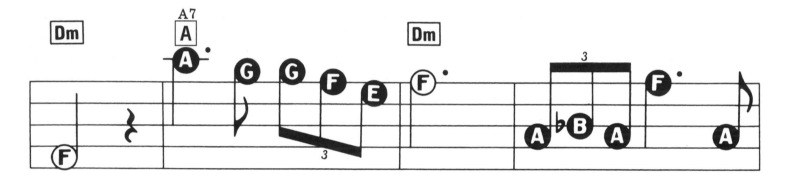

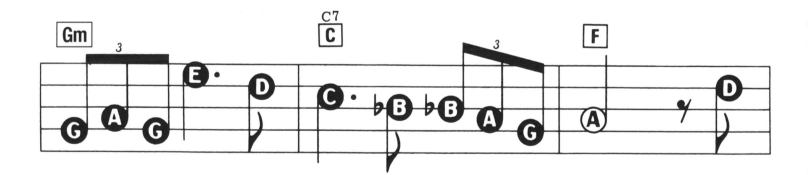

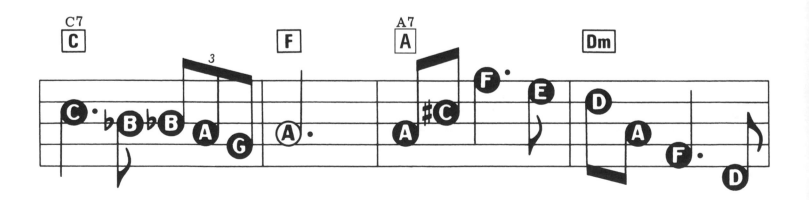

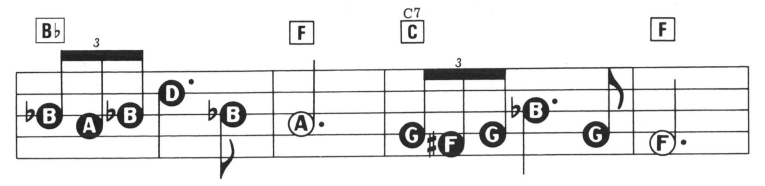

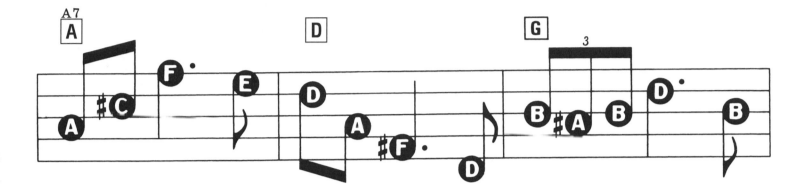

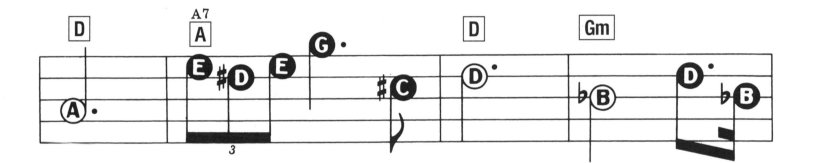

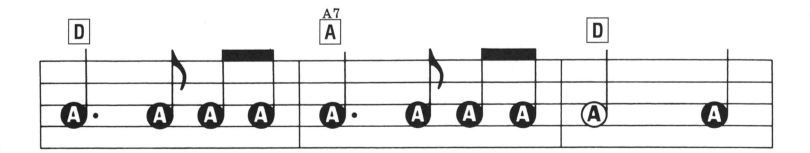

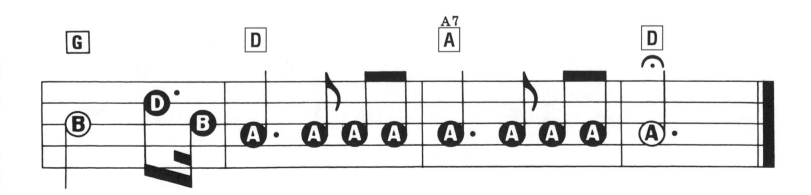

The Skaters
(Waltz)

Registration 5
Rhythm: Waltz

By Emil Waldteufel

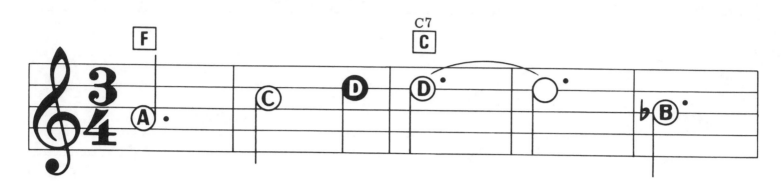

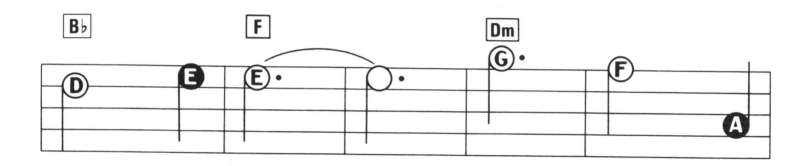

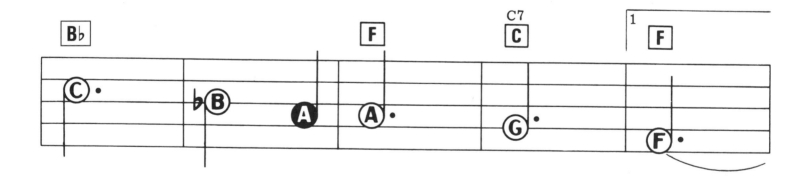

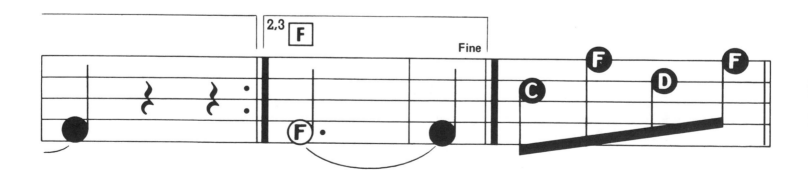

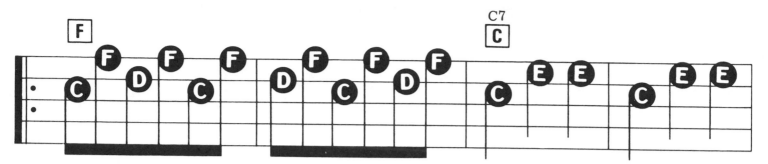

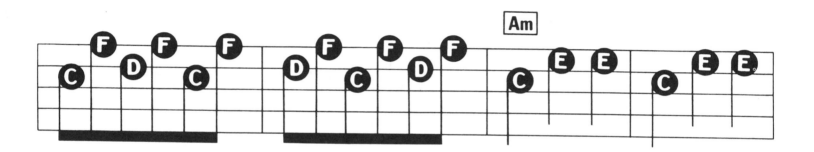

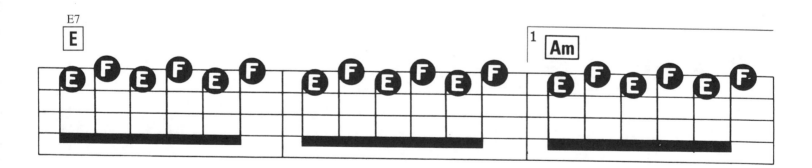

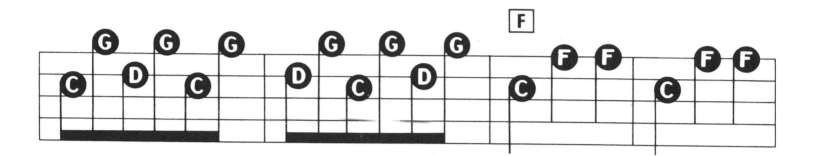

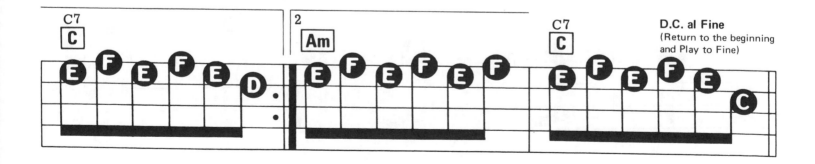

Tales from the Vienna Woods

Registration 4
Rhythm: Fox Trot

By Johann Strauss, Jr.

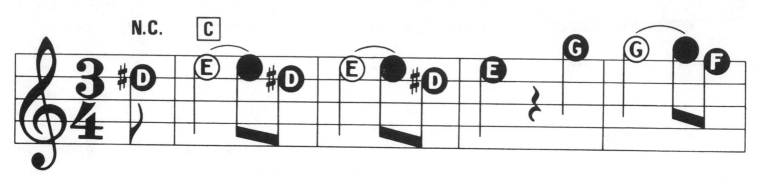

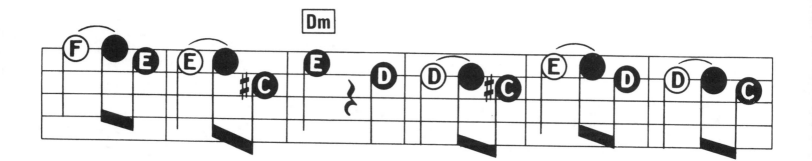

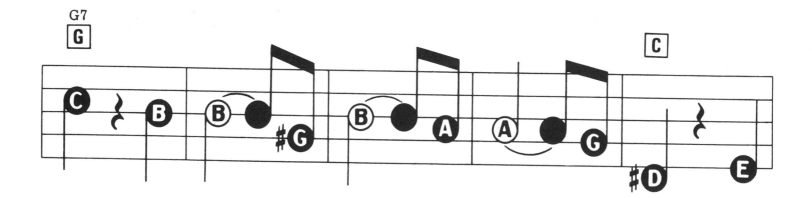

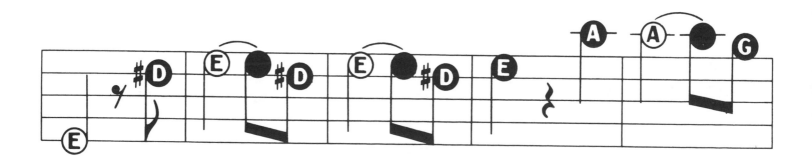

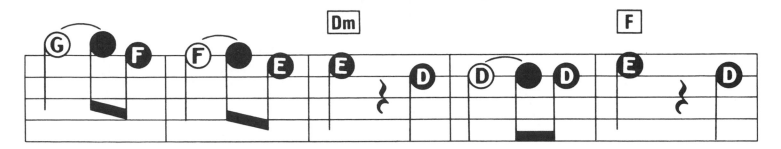

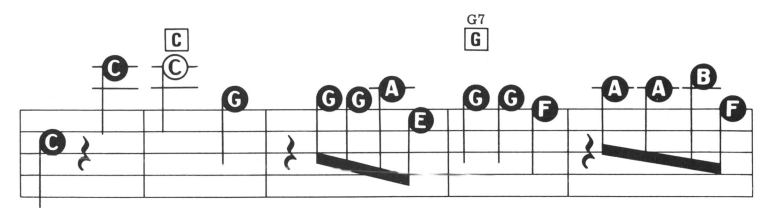

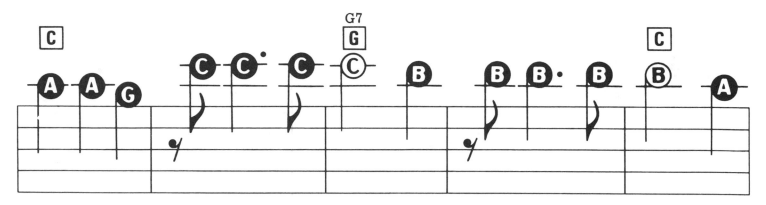

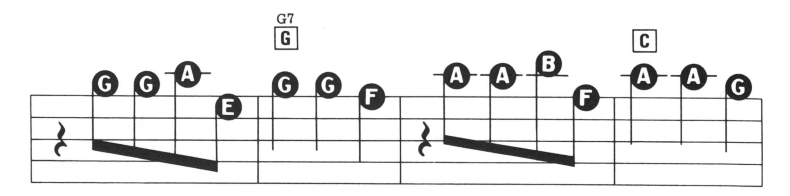

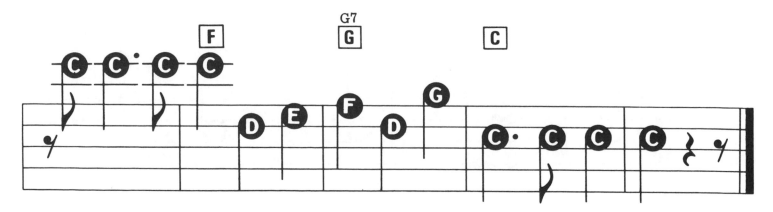

Toreador Song
from CARMEN

Registration 1
Rhythm: March

By Georges Bizet

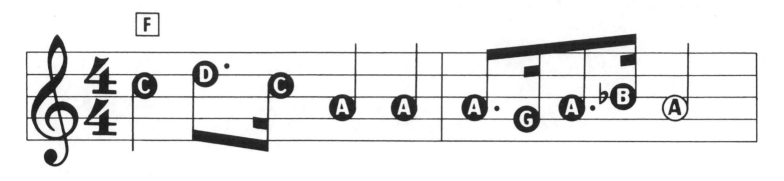

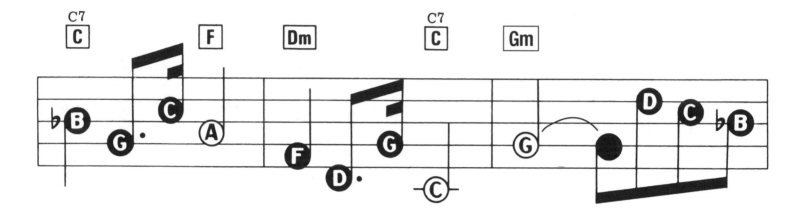

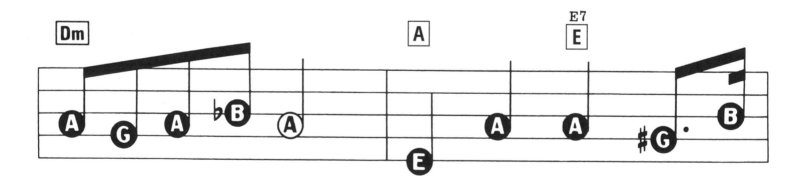

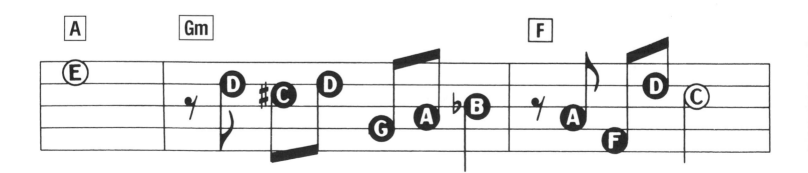

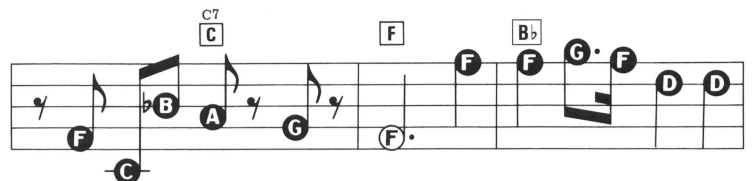

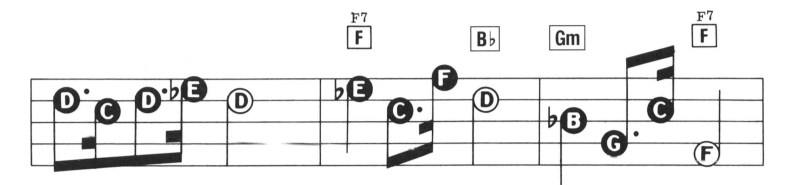

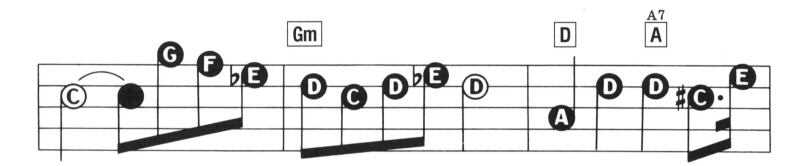

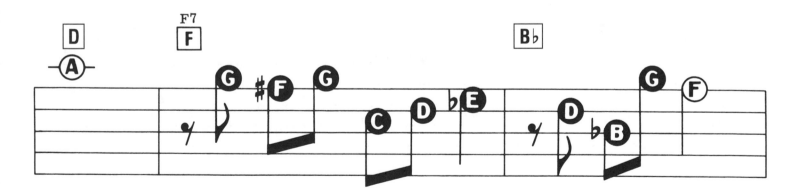

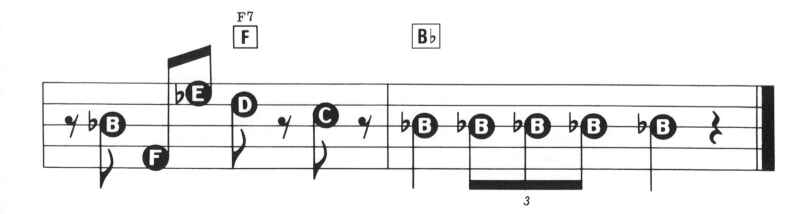

Triumphal March
from AIDA

Registration 2
Rhythm: March

By Giuseppe Verdi

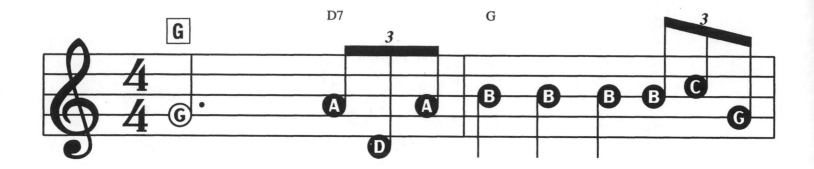

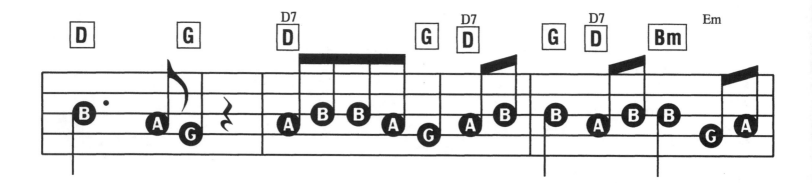

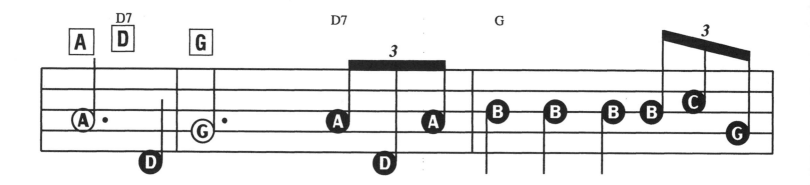

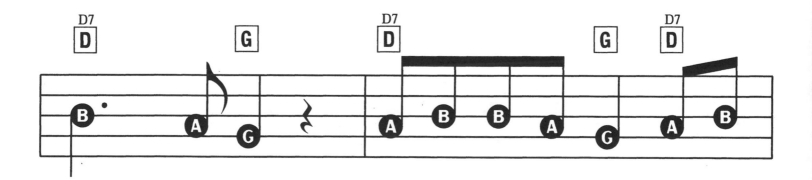

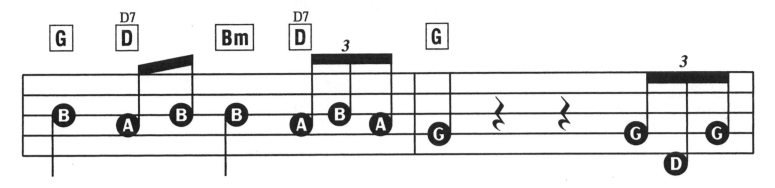

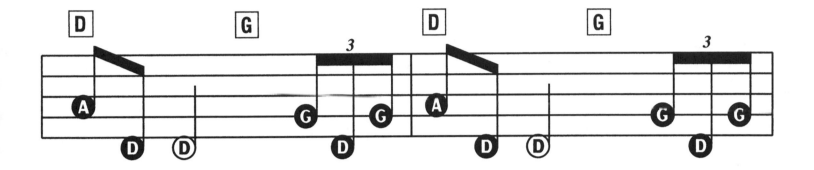

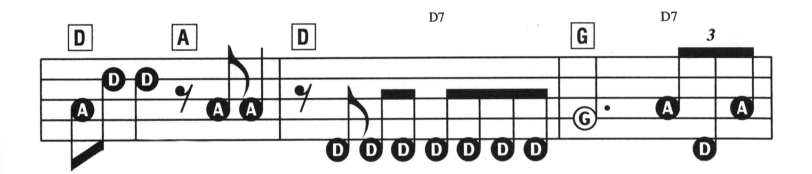

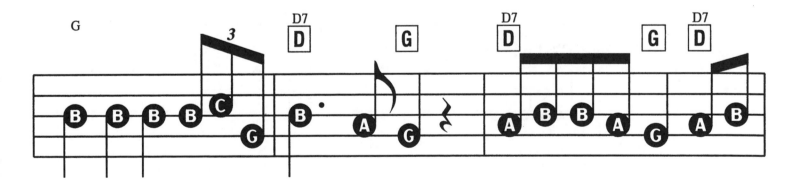

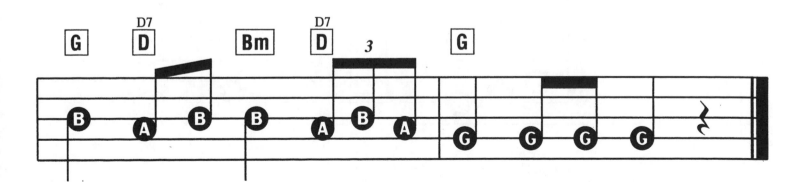

Valse Bleue

Registration 3
Rhythm: Waltz

By Alfred Margis

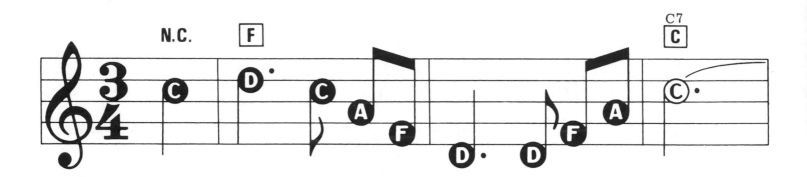

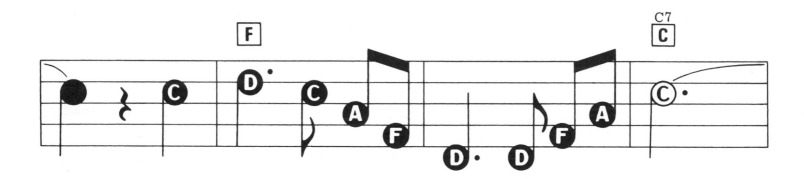

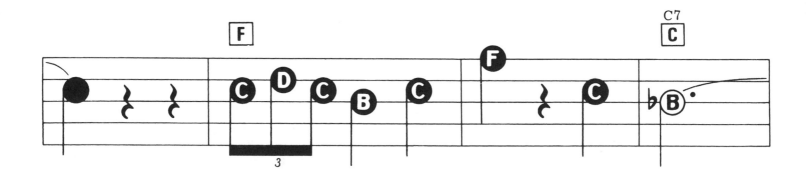

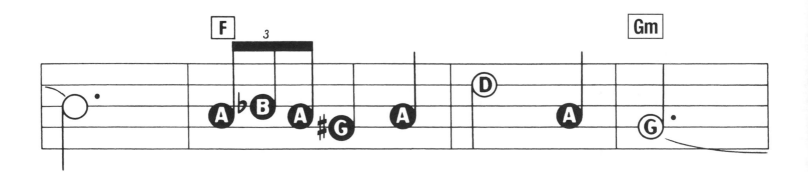

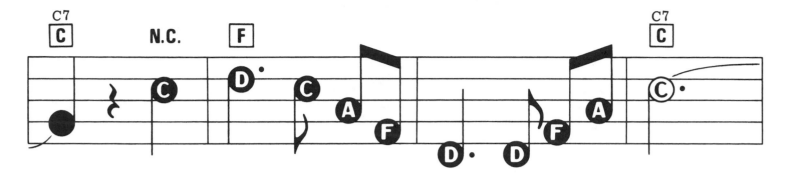

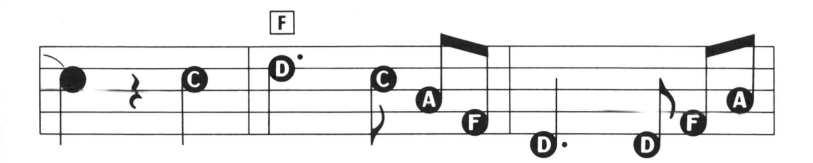

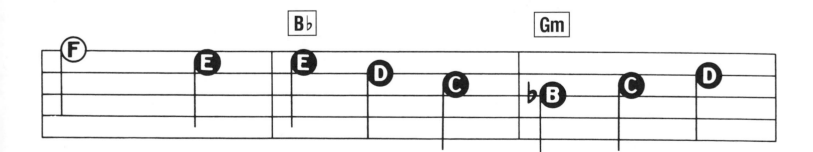

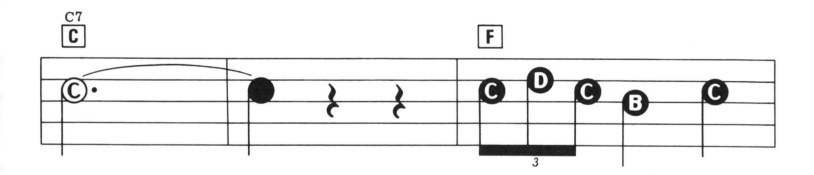

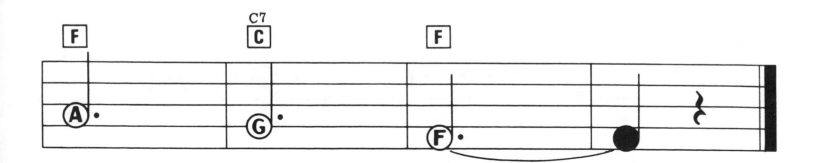

Vienna Life

Registration 3
Rhythm: Waltz

By Johann Straus, Jr.

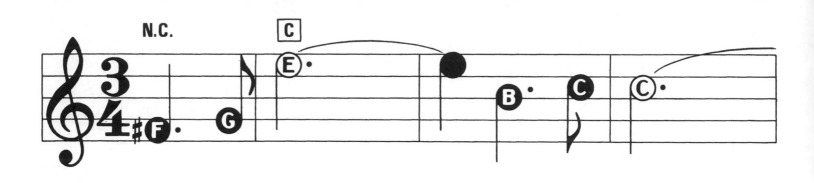

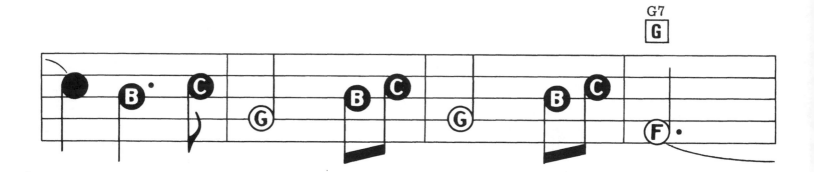

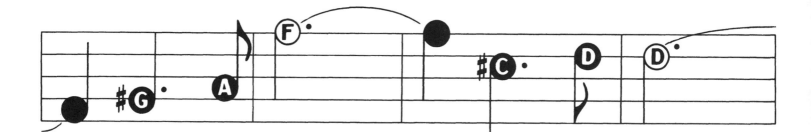

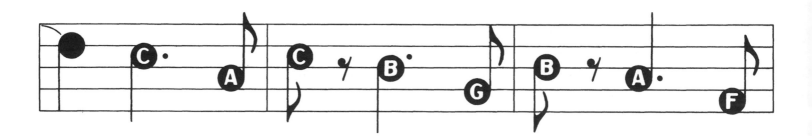

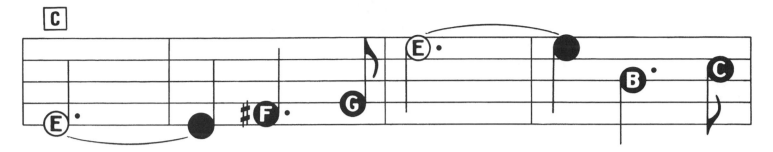

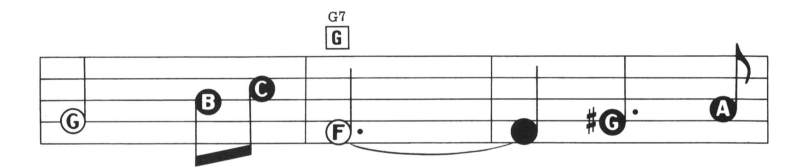

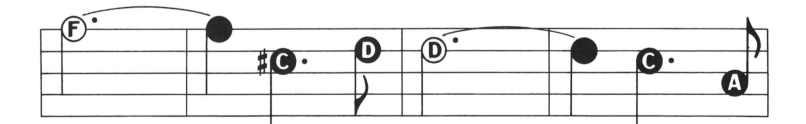

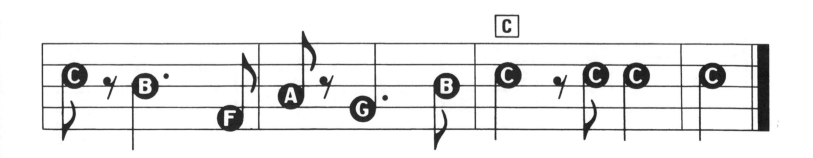

Waltz
from THE WALTZ DREAM

Registration 1
Rhythm: Waltz

By Oscar Straus

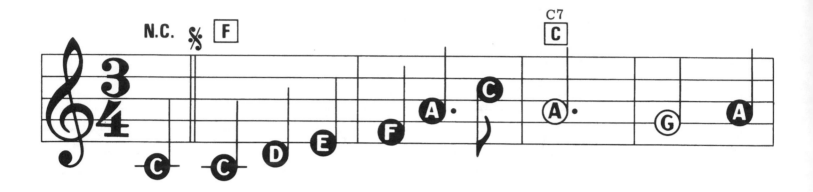

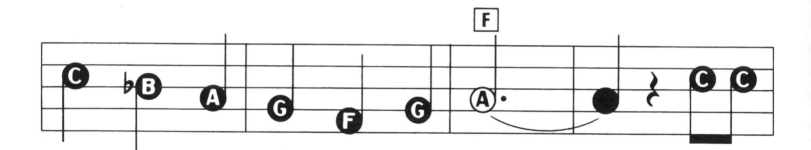

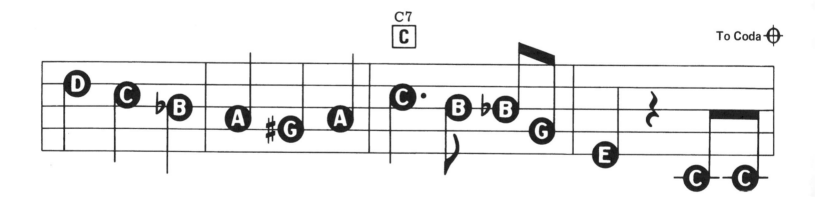

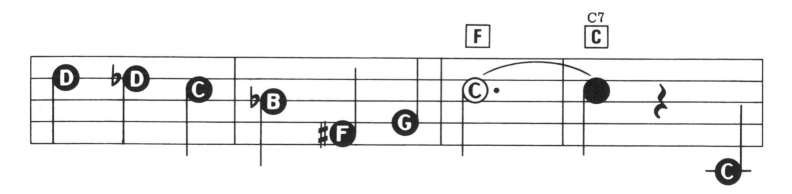

63

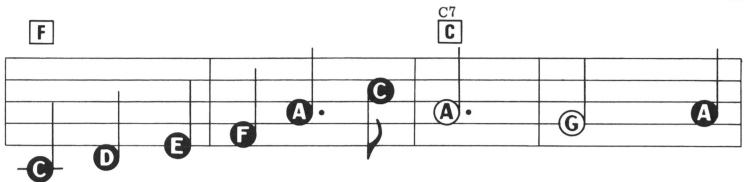

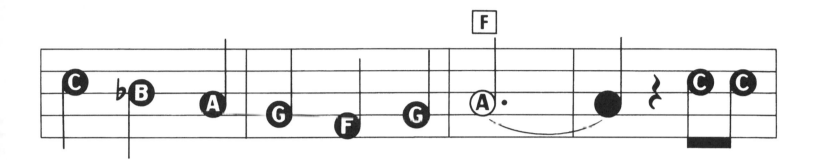

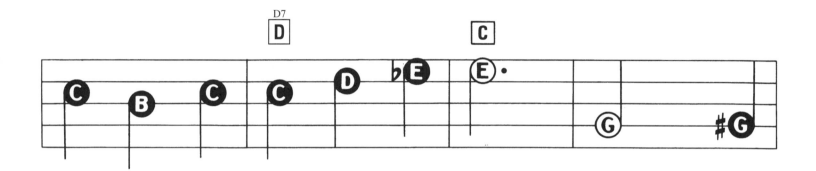

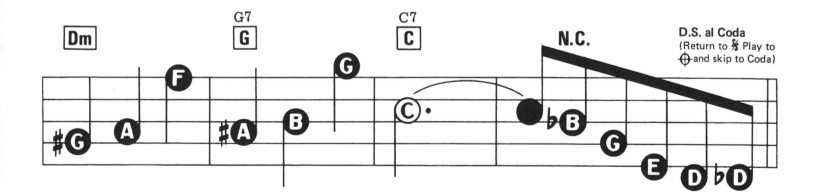

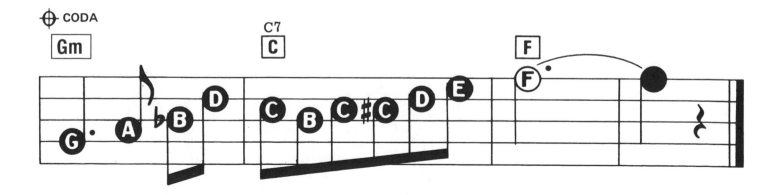

 # Registration Guide

• Match the Registration number on the song to the corresponding numbered category below. Select and activate an instrumental sound available on your instrument.

• Choose an automatic rhythm appropriate to the mood and style of the song. (Consult your Owner's Guide for proper operation of automatic rhythm features.)

• Adjust the tempo and volume controls to comfortable settings.

Registration

1	Mellow	Flutes, Clarinet, Oboe, Flugel Horn, Trombone, French Horn, Organ Flutes
2	Ensemble	Brass Section, Sax Section, Wind Ensemble, Full Organ, Theater Organ
3	Strings	Violin, Viola, Cello, Fiddle, String Ensemble, Pizzicato, Organ Strings
4	Guitars	Acoustic/Electric Guitars, Banjo, Mandolin, Dulcimer, Ukulele, Hawaiian Guitar
5	Mallets	Vibraphone, Marimba, Xylophone, Steel Drums, Bells, Celesta, Chimes
6	Liturgical	Pipe Organ, Hand Bells, Vocal Ensemble, Choir, Organ Flutes
7	Bright	Saxophones, Trumpet, Mute Trumpet, Synth Leads, Jazz/Gospel Organs
8	Piano	Piano, Electric Piano, Honky Tonk Piano, Harpsichord, Clavi
9	Novelty	Melodic Percussion, Wah Trumpet, Synth, Whistle, Kazoo, Perc. Organ
10	Bellows	Accordion, French Accordion, Mussette, Harmonica, Pump Organ, Bagpipes